LIFE Surrendered

FINDING FREEDOM AT THE CROSS

JESSICA HERBERGER

LEAFWOOD
PUBLISHERS
an imprint of Abilene Christian University Press

LIFE SURRENDERED

Finding Freedom at the Cross

LEAFWOOD
PUBLISHERS
an imprint of Abilene Christian University Press

ISBN 978-1-68426-491-9

Printed in the United States of America

Published in association with The Blythe Daniel Agency, Inc., PO Box 64197, Colorado Springs, CO 80962.

Cataloging-in-Publication Data is on file at the Library of Congress, Washington, DC.

Cover design by Bruce Gore
Interior text design by Sandy Armstrong, Strong Design

Leafwood Publishers is an imprint of Abilene Christian University Press
ACU Box 29138
Abilene, Texas 79699

1-877-816-4455
www.leafwoodpublishers.com

22 23 24 25 26 27 28 / 7 6 5 4 3 2 1

LIFE Surrendered

"In *Life Surrendered*, Jessica Herberger leads us along the way of suffering and draws us into Jesus's last hours wrapped in humanity. We are asked to pause and consider how our own grief has shaped and is shaping our faith—an invitation Jessica, who has known deep grief, participates in alongside us. This moving account of Good Friday carries a gentle yet powerful message for the season of loss so many of us are living."

—**Deborah Beddoe,** author of *The Heart of Recovery*

"Jessica Herberger plumbs the depths of liberty and grace found in opening our clenched fists and yielding our lives fully to the redemptive work of Jesus Christ. As she walks with us through the biblical account of Good Friday—the crucifixion, death, and burial of Jesus—Jess wraps each moment in flesh-and-bone personality. We consider the fight found in Peter, the anguish of Judas, the care provided Mary in the midst of the heartbreak. Each chapter offers a welcoming space for reflection and confession as we are invited to reconsider our perspective on what we value and what we hold dear."

—**Ronne Rock,** long-road walker and author of *One Woman Can Change the World*

"Through her words and life, with an eye for God in the details, Jessica Herberger once again shows us that nothing was or is coincidental on the way to the cross. *Life Surrendered* beautifully weaves familiar scripture with fascinating historical details, insightful theology, and personal experience, taking readers on an open-handed journey through Good Friday to freedom found in Christ. The depths and 'deaths' of Good Friday examined in this book will change you."

—**Amy Morgan,** author, speaker, and cofounder of Seasons Northeast

"It's tempting for Christians to skip over the agony of Christ's passion, to race ahead to the gladness of Easter morning, yet our souls need to learn the lessons of the path to the cross. With deep faith and intimate knowledge of both life and death, Jessica Herberger is a trustworthy guide as we journey with Jesus. Her kind but firm words challenge and bless. I highly recommend *Life Surrendered*."

—**Richella J. Parham,** author of *Mythical Me* and cohost of *Friends in Formation*

"In a time when the world seems obsessed with celebrity and influence, Jessica Herberger writes as a disciple. Her ability to climb inside scriptures as both learner and guide results in work that is at once authentic, wise, insightful, and challenging. While pop culture would have us believe surrender equates to defeat, Jessica demonstrates that surrender before Jesus brings freedom."

—**Adriel Booker,** author of *Grace Like Scarlett* and host of *Tethered* and *Our Scarlett Stories*

"In the tradition of Dietrich Bonhoeffer's *Cost of Discipleship* and Andrew Murray's *Absolute Surrender*, Jessica Herberger challenges Christians to embrace a biblical vision of Christian surrender. Grounded in the Passion narratives of the Gospels, *Life Surrendered* calls the reader to move from shallow believism to a radical expression of what it means to walk the Way of Jesus the way Jesus walked the Way. *Life Surrendered* is faithful to God's Word, relevant to the difficult challenges people face in daily life, and rooted in a historic understanding of genuine relinquishment. Jessica Herberger has given us a gift, refocusing our eyes and hearts upon the freedom that comes to us by way of the Cross of Christ."

—**Terry Wardle,** Founder, Healing Care Ministries, and author of many books, including *From Broken to Beloved*

For Osh

and the many deaths we faced together

CONTENTS

ACKNOWLEDGMENTS

Writing this book has been like plumbing the depths. Each time I came up for air, I was greeted with kindness and care, and for that I am eternally grateful.

Amy—you say I am your biggest cheerleader, but the opposite is actually true. It's you for me. You are steadfast and faithful at personal cost that not many see. I am so honored to call you friend.

Renée—this book is for you as much as it is for me. May we continue to let go, together. God knew how much we would need each other, and I am thankful for that.

Adriel—your friendship is one of the great unexpected gifts of this season. You spur me on to do better work. I am incredibly grateful for your voice in my life.

To the writers in my life who encourage me—particularly The Writers Bloc, my Voxer group, Adriel, Ronne, KJ, and Lore—your welcome and wisdom continually shape me.

Caleb Peavy—this book would never have come to be so swiftly without your guidance in launching BBT so well. I'm grateful for your generous sharing of wisdom and your equipping me to keep going and steward this message well.

Community Prayer Group—look at what God has done and keeps doing when we simply show up for each other. So grateful he gave me this group to pray with. Thank you for your faithful obedience.

LCC—it is a rare thing to have come out of the last two years prouder of your church than you were before, yet that is my reality. I truly love our church; and even more so, I love who we are becoming. Particular gratitude goes to Pastors Paul and Mike, who have offered support, wisdom, and guidance throughout the rapid forming of this book.

Leafwood—I have never been more certain of being with exactly the right team of people. Jason and Duane, your partnership allows me to be faithful in this work. I am grateful for your expertise and your encouragement. Mary, your stewardship of this project and your partnership has been a gift!

To our lake family—where the mountains and lake meet is a haven that not many in this world truly understand. When a place and people hold so many memories, there is a particular kind of magic that reminds us of heaven.

Maxson, Elise, and Finley—thank you for accepting that God has a few more books for Mom to write and for surrendering to that with grace and excitement well beyond your years. You are each so loved and so special.

Josh—thank you for the countless ways you support everything I do. For delighting in every success. For being the soft place I get to land. Every best day is with you.

INTRODUCTION

This is a book about death. Admittedly, that's a funny way to begin a book about life. One of the great lessons I have learned over time is that all of life is tied up in death. Living life well requires us to die daily. In Christian circles, we call this death to self. It is not a new concept, of course, yet it is one we do not willingly step into. Not all the way.

I yearn to die to self yet am constantly grasping for control. I claim to trust God yet hold tightly to things such as my schedule, my entitlement, my reputation. I want to let these things die, yet so often I hold on to them for dear life. This is the tension Good Friday addresses. Over and over from the moment in the garden to the last moments at the tomb, we see a letting go and a surrendering to God's way—death after death after death throughout the day. Death to self is like that. It is a letting go, an opening of those clenched fists. It is an affirmation over and over again that God's way leads to freedom. But it requires death.

Rev. Jean-Pierre De Caussade confirms this connection between life and death: "In the path of pure faith, all that takes place spiritually, physically, and temporarily, has the aspect of death."[1]

Our willingness to lay down our control, to live surrendered, is what will allow us to be formed in a way that only God can achieve. It allows us to live a life of freedom—the freedom bought for us on the cross.

Walking with Jesus through Good Friday is a heavy exercise. There is hope at every turn, but there is also a weight to it that can feel overwhelming. My appeal to you is to stick with it. I felt this weight profoundly as I wrote this book, spending over a year on the road from Gethsemane to Golgotha. The heaviness was palpable at times, yet this is part of the journey of death. I believe you, like I, will arrive at the end of this good day, Good Friday, with a profound sense of freedom. May you welcome each death along the way.

---

[1]Jean-Pierre De Caussade, *Abandonment to Divine Providence* (New York: Cosimo Classics, 2007).

PART ONE

Foundations of Freedom

As we begin the day of Good Friday, we meet Jesus in the Garden of Gethsemane uttering those words we all know so well, "Not my will, but yours" (Luke 22:42). Yet what does that really mean for us today? If we are to live a life surrendered, it starts here—laying it all down.

The very notion of the passion of Christ is wrapped up in his laying it all down. To our modern sensibilities, the word *passion* conjures images of intensity, excitement, and energy. Passion sounds active—something you do or express. Yet this passion, the passion we see on Good Friday, is the opposite of that. Passion, as used to describe what Jesus did on Good Friday, comes from the Latin word *passio*, which means "passivity." As Ronald Rolheiser wrote in his impactful book on spiritual maturity, *Sacred Fire*, "He gives his death to us through his passivity, just as he had previously given his life to us through his activity."[1]

We are called to live out deaths every day as a means of drawing us closer to the passivity we see in Christ—his willingness to lay everything aside as he seeks the Father's will. This is the foundation of the freedom he shows us at the cross. And it all begins, as it often does, in a garden.

---

[1]Ronald Rolheiser, *Sacred Fire: A Vision for a Deeper Human and Christian Maturity* (New York: Doubleday, 2017).

CHAPTER ONE

THE FREEDOM OF RELEASING CONTROL

Death of Self

Jesus Prays in the Garden

Matthew 26:36–46 | Mark 14:32–42 | Luke 22:39–46

I am a fist clencher. I may joke that I am a control freak, but that badge is not one I truly want to own. I can change the narrative in my own mind to bring comfort: *There is no one else to take over. I am the best person suited to lead. I know how to get us out of this. I am unafraid to step in.* While certainly this type of thinking can have positive effects when kept in check, in reality it's mostly unnecessary. Here's what I really am: *I am a fist clencher.*

I have clenched my fists, in my sleep no less, so tightly that I have woken up with cuts on my palms from my own fingernails. During some particularly high-stress seasons of my life, I have slept holding a sock in each hand as a way to protect myself from myself. Ouch. Throughout the day, I often find myself opening my palms wide to release the self-inflicted tension. I have learned that if I want to remain open and peace-filled during difficult conversations, I can sit with my hands open, placed on my lap. And then as my disloyal fingers begin to curl back up again, I know to stop and breathe and release once more.

Maybe you don't clench your fists. Maybe your shoulders tend to migrate north up to your ears; maybe you grit your teeth, bite your nails, stop eating, overeat, tap your feet, clean and scour every surface—there is a massive list of all the ways our wrestle with control can manifest in our lives.

In the face of crisis, it's important to spend some time considering what our response to stress and control is. These simple gestures can be a signal to us that what we say we feel may not be indicative of what is actually going on with our minds and spirits. I was in a veterinarian's office the first time I realized I was not all that attuned to my inner thoughts and stress levels. I was in my early twenties at the time, gainfully employed and on a very successful and enjoyable career tract, settled with my spouse and our beloved German Shorthaired Pointer, Gunther. Things seemed to be going along just swimmingly. But for some reason, I was having moments of blacking out. These episodes had escalated to the point that I was wearing a Holter monitor so the doctors could sort out what was going on. Ultimately, I was given a clean bill of health and told that the episodes were a stress response.

Stress response?! How could that be when I wasn't even stressed?! I brushed this obviously foolish assessment aside and moved on with my week. Fast-forward to the vet's office, where I stood next to our sweet pup and was told that he likely had a disease that would cause a short life span and great suffering to his body. Just to be perfectly clear, Gunther was *everything* to us. He was our firstborn baby. I had never cared for another the way I cared for Gunther. To hear this news was devastating. As the vet continued on, the room closed in, went dark, and down I went. Stress response. Turns out my body was worn out from my tendency to constantly push through life—controlling it all—and then when I was confronted with my actual lack of control . . . I blacked out.

That moment was the first moment in what has been a continual wrestling with God, of laying down my desire for control and forging ahead, at any cost, to what I see as good. I had a white-knuckle grip on my life, and when what I was holding still managed to slip through my fingers, I became undone. But it was in the undoing that I finally began to understand that what I perceive as the best course of action does not always line up with God's best. And that's okay.

The true best, God's best, is the path to freedom and abundance. This is not a prosperity gospel type of promise but instead an invitation to imagine that freedom and abundance can exist amid the hardships of this life.

The incident with Gunther, who by the way went on to live a long and wonderful life full of swimming and ball chasing and general goofiness, was my introduction to the concept that life may not go as planned. In the vet's office that day, I came face-to-face with the sobering concept that in a moment, things could change drastically. I have lived that reality out dozens of times since then. Over the last twenty years, I have seen what happens when we trust God's best for our lives. It is heartbreakingly beautiful.

When we release control and instead trust that God will meet us and lead us to his best, we are given a whole new way of living. There may be death, but there is also life. This is Good Friday—heartbreakingly beautiful.

The first hours of Good Friday find Jesus in the garden, known as Gethsemane or the Mount of Olives, as he wrestles with the reality of the death and darkness he is about to face. We all know the words Jesus utters here, "Not my will, but yours" (Luke 22:42). But, despite our familiarity with the scene, I still think it is important to linger here in the garden.

It was late in the evening hours. Jesus and the disciples had just departed from their Passover celebration. Scholars estimate it was around 10:00 p.m. as they settled in. Jesus asks the disciples to stay and remain on guard, and he beckons three, Peter, James, and John, to keep an even closer watch as he prays to the Father.

As Jesus leaves the three to pray, he tells them his soul is grieved and full of sorrow (Matt. 26:38). Anytime I find myself clenching my fists, this is exactly what is going on inside me. Like Christ, I am grieved and full of sorrow.

As Jesus steps away to pray, we hear those words that we know so well: "Going a little farther, he fell facedown and prayed, 'My Father, if it is possible, let this cup pass from me. Yet not as I will, but as you will'" (Matt. 26:39).

The cup that Jesus references is the cup of God's wrath and judgment. Throughout Scripture, we see the cup used to symbolize this, with a foretelling in Isaiah 51:17 of this particular cup of God's fury that Jesus faces. Jesus knows what is coming. And in desperation, he asks if there is another way.

I believe this instance shows Christ as fully human responding to what seems unfathomable, incredibly difficult, so overwhelming, bringing grief and sorrow upon him that already feels like death itself. Have you been there?

My Gethsemane was found in Room One of the Emergency Department at St. Peter's Hospital. Within the hospital ED and ICU, there is a ranking of critical needs that is reflected in the room placement. You never want to be in Room One—the top case, the most critical. Yet there I stood, at my mom's bedside. She had what we assumed was a stroke earlier that day. She was nonresponsive, and her blood pressure was through the roof. They had just taken her for a brain scan. My dad was seated in the corner of the tiny room, a stroke victim in his own right. His stroke, eleven years earlier, had left him unable to drive or work, with consistent seizures, and struggling with balance, verbal processing, and comprehension, among other challenges. As we sat there, staring at my mom, he was silent, concerned, and confused. I braced for the results from the scans, imagining life with two stroke victims.

The doctor whipped into the room, scan reports in hand, and rapidly said in a disconnected, cold tone, "There is a large mass in her brain." The words fell off his lips so casually, as if the entire world had not just crashed around my feet. The large mass, we would learn, was a glioblastoma multiforme (GBM), one of the most invasive, hard-to-treat types of brain tumors. As quickly as he walked in, the doctor walked out. There were no comforting words offered, no plan or next steps. He just dropped the bomb in the room and moved on.

At that moment, I could only cry out, in a faint whisper, "No, no, no." This could not be the way for us. *Please, God, could there be another way?* I was prepared for a stroke, but a terminal brain tumor seemed impossible. I was deeply grieved, to the point of death itself. Life, as I thought it would be, had died, and the doctor had so carelessly delivered the death sentence.

I am thankful for that moment in the Garden of Gethsemane, with Jesus crying out, asking for another way. We can find so much fellowship in that moment, which serves to not only demonstrate the humanness of Christ but also offer us true communion with him as we too cry out, "Is there another way?"

Just as Jesus acknowledges in Mark 14:36 that "all things are possible for you," we too acknowledge that our very asking honors the truth that God is capable of changing our circumstances. This is why we cry out. We cry out because we confess God's omnipotence. We cry out to God because there is no one more powerful, more caring, or more secure to go to. If you have ever believed the opposite, if in your crying out you have ever felt shame or humiliation, if you have ever believed that begging for a different outcome indicates a faith that is lacking, simply look at Jesus in Gethsemane.

Here, Jesus makes the request three times. His hours spent in the garden weren't simply a brief moment of weakened faith. This was an ongoing dialogue with the Lord, seeking God's will, asking again and again for another way. In your crying out, find comfort and communion with Jesus.

Only after petitioning the Lord does Jesus then say, "But not my will, yours." Jesus relents to God's will, acknowledging that the outcome is worthy and good simply because it is God's will. We now know what the outcome was, the finished work of bearing God's wrath so that all may have salvation and justification in the eyes of God. This is, of course, an outcome worthy of great celebration. But don't confuse the story of Easter with the story of Good Friday. Good Friday is about the pain and suffering, the unjust persecution, the betrayal of friends, the pain of those who mourn. And, yet, we call it "Good." The good is simply because it was God's will.

How can death be good? How can suffering be good? This is the tension of Good Friday. This is what makes letting go of control so hard. We don't want to invite death and suffering into our lives. Yet, here on the Mount of Olives, Jesus shows us another way to live—the living that comes from letting go of control, of welcoming God's will into our lives, is one of freedom, even freedom to the point of death.

This letting go, the welcoming of God's will in your life, is a solitary exercise. No one can open your clenched palms for you. There is no friend who can welcome God's will into your life. No one can lay down your life but *you*. And yet, our friends, our community, do have a role to play in our letting go.

Go back to the garden—the disciples and Jesus had just left the Last Supper. The evening of the Last Supper is a master class of friendship and community. It lays out the high call of friendship for believers. Jesus prays for oneness among them that is the same as the oneness he has with the Father. All this to say, Jesus takes this very seriously.

It is striking then that Jesus asks Peter, James, and John to keep watch a distance from where he was praying. From this, we can see the role of our deepest friends in these moments of wrestling with God, of releasing the things we cling to in an effort to gain control. Our friends are called to be the watchmen. We, as friends, are called to be watchmen.

The Greek word Jesus uses, *menō*, also translates as the word "abide." "Remain here and stay awake" (Mark 14:34). We are called to stand watch as our friends lay their lives before God. We must invite them into that place in our own lives. As we have things to lay down before him, we must do it on our own, but we are also able to have friends stand guard for us.

The frustration, of course, comes when our friends are not as faithful to their posts as they could be. We certainly see that in Gethsemane as well. I am humbled to see that upon his discovery of the sleeping watchmen, Jesus does not simply give up on them. He instead wakes them up and once again calls them to their post. This demonstrates both the importance of having those watchmen in our lives and also the reality that they will likely not be faithful to their posts. This is not an example of how we can move on from them, or how inconsequential these friends are. Instead, it is a call for us to stay with them and they with us. Abide. Stay. *Menō*.

Now here is where it gets really interesting. Jesus encourages the three to stay awake—to keep watch and pray so that they won't fall into temptation (Matt. 26:41; Mark 14:38). *Temptation* in this context refers to a testing that will come for each of them. Jesus is therefore asserting that in their watching and standing with him as he lays down his will in favor of the Father's, they will be edified for their own testing and temptations. Friends, as we each lay down our need for control, as we each pursue the Father's will in our lives, we encourage and equip others to do the same. This is why Jesus continues to wake the disciples up! It is as if he is saying, "Don't miss this!" Don't miss the opportunity to be formed in this specific way, to be edified and emboldened so that when it is our turn to lay down our control, we will already be equipped by having witnessed others doing the same.

Jesus affirms that while our spirits may be willing, our flesh is weak (Matt. 26:41; Mark 14:38). When our spirit is yearning to let go and our hands remain clenched, it is the witnessing of others' trust in God's will that will push us to do the same.

This is the beauty of the kingdom.

As we begin to walk through the hours of Good Friday, may we begin by laying down any sense that our will is the best way. May we understand that the fight for letting go of control and saying with confidence, "Not my will, but yours," is an exchange solely between God and ourselves. We must be willing to stand up from Gethsemane, confident in God's good will for us, even when it looks like death, knowing that life truly begins there. As Jesus said to the disciples, "Get up; let's go" (Mark 14:42). There is a life of beauty waiting for us. May we welcome the letting go.

Via Dolorosa Way of Grief

As we follow Jesus from Gethsemane to Golgotha and then to the tomb, take a few moments to sit quietly with him. Similar to the Way of the Cross or Stations of the Cross, we will pause to reflect on the moments and meaning of Good Friday. There is grief in death. But there is also grief in our sin and in our misalignment with God. Before we continue on, we must pause and grieve.

REFLECT

- Where are you grasping on to control?
- As you reflect, ask God to reveal his presence and will. What does he show you?

CONFESS

- Have you condemned yourself for crying out?
- Have you placed watchmen in your life?
- Where is there misalignment in your desires, actions, and thoughts?
- Where are you not valuing what Jesus valued?

RECONSIDER

- Letting go of our will and seeking God's will is the way to freedom, beauty, and life.
- The redemptive work begins with letting go of control.
- Take time to pray and affirm this.

CHAPTER TWO

LETTING GO OF THE BATTLES THAT AREN'T YOURS

Death of the Fight

Jesus Arrested | Peter Strikes the Servant Malchus

Matthew 26:51–54 | Mark 14:47–52 | Luke 22:49–52 | John 18:10–11

I am a fighter. In the stereotypical Challenger mentality,[1] I am energized by the pushback, by anyone strong enough to stay in the ring with me for a few rounds. This energy, as I continue to mature in Christ, has been channeled for good. But that hasn't always been the case.

I used to be a launch, confront, fight, then check-for-the-collateral-damage kind of challenger. Not pretty. I would forge ahead with my plan relentlessly. My confidence overtook my conscience more times than I care to recall.

[1]This refers to the Enneagram types. The description for a type eight (which is what I am) is often Challenger. We eights are known for our propensity to fight.

Even when I found myself fighting what seemed to be the "good fight," I didn't know if I was engaged in a battle that was mine to fight or if perhaps I had stepped in out of turn. But, honestly, that didn't much matter to me. A good fight won was a victory, no matter the price, no matter the outcome. It never occurred to me that perhaps I was too eager to fight. Perhaps I had lost, or never sought, an awareness of which fights God was calling me to—and the ones he had not set aside for me.

Here is what I have learned: what looks brave and bold may actually be blind, brazen foolishness.

For those of us who like the fight, or are energized by a challenge, we stand in real danger of playing the fool. What can appear to be dedication, perseverance, and stick-to-itiveness may truly be us imposing our will, a stubborn, my-way-or-the-highway attitude bent on manifesting our will, without regard for God's plan.

As we continue to press into this concept of letting go of control, of honoring and inviting God's will into our lives, we must take a look at the fights we pick and the hills we choose to climb. Letting a fight die, laying it down unfinished or even seemingly defeated, may be exactly the way you can experience the fullest life Jesus can offer. This is not throwing in the towel or taking the easy way out. This is a hard path to follow. In fact, for many of us, myself included, this may be the biggest challenge of Good Friday—knowing when to let go of the fight.

There is a tremendous amount of discernment required here. The wisdom and discernment needed only comes from spending time with God—ideally before you are in the fray. It can be as simple as asking him.

But why is it so hard to just bring myself to ask God for the spirit of discernment in my life? I think the unflattering answer goes back to my enjoyment of the fight. And by *fight* I mean any battle, campaign, mission, or quest I can find myself on. This is why we, the fighters in particular, are obliged to be even more careful to be in tune with God before we step in. If we aren't careful, we, like Peter, could be in danger of blocking or forgetting God's sovereignty.

A few notes before we dive into this next round of Scripture: First, there are some scenes on Good Friday that are a bit gruesome; this is one of them. Second, the Gospel accounts of Matthew, Mark, and Luke do not specifically identify Peter as the one who cut off the ear of the servant (Malchus). However, John *does* clearly identify him. When the first three accounts were written, Peter was still alive and therefore this offense could have been used against him, even years after the event. In contrast, John's Gospel was written much later, after Peter was martyred and therefore no such threat existed.

We are still in the Garden of Gethsemane. It's dark. There is a large group approaching. I've always pictured Judas and a handful of men with some torches. In reality, there was a band of men: a cohort of either six hundred legionnaires or a thousand auxiliary soldiers; a captain (the Greek word is *chiliarchos*, which literally means a commander of a thousand soldiers); officers from the chief priests and Pharisees; and, yes, Judas—all coming with torches, lanterns, and weapons. This was no small group, and Peter was ready to jump into the fray.

> At that moment one of those with Jesus reached out his hand and drew his sword. He struck the high priest's servant and cut off his ear. Then Jesus told him, "Put your sword back in its place because all who take up the sword will perish by the sword. Or do you think that I cannot call on my Father, and he will provide me here and now with more than twelve legions of angels? How,

> then, would the Scriptures be fulfilled that say it must happen this way?" (Matt. 26:51–54)

If I had to guess, I believe my old friend Peter was a Challenger. But also, what was he thinking?!

The assumption is that Peter was looking to attack and distract so that Jesus could escape. He was willingly walking into harm's way. The numbers are staggering when you consider at best the ratio was 1,000:11. While it may be our first inclination to admire his bravery, remember that what looks like brave action can often be brazen foolishness.

Jesus's response is what we must consider here: he admonishes Peter, he points him back to the full power and autonomy of God, and then he heals the wounded.

First, he admonishes Peter. Jesus immediately calls out Peter's attack as wrong. Clearly, this was a misjudgment on Peter's part. In Matthew 26:52, we see Jesus condemn the use of the sword and warn that those who take up their swords will perish from the same. The act of fighting, even defending, violently is called out by Jesus as a path to death.

Next, he reminds Peter of the available power of God. If there was an actual battle to fight, God is more powerful than any group of men and more than ready to step in. Do we believe that? If we quickly step into every fight, ready to do the work from our own strength, what does that say about our belief in God's power? What does it say about our belief in God's willingness to intercede on our behalf?

Then, Jesus heals the servant's ear (Luke 22:51). This was the last miracle of Jesus before his death on the cross, and while it was of course kind of him to heal his enemy, I believe that miracle was ultimately for Peter. The consequence for attacking Malchus would have been devastating to Peter personally and to the disciples as a group. Their very safety would have been in question. But, even more so, Peter's actions were going to block the fulfillment of Scripture, and this could not happen.

Jesus was keenly aware of the cup he must drink; he was also aware that he had just finished praying to the Father that he had "not lost one of those you have given me" (John 18:9). And had Peter been arrested or worse, the words Jesus spoke would have been negated. Peter would not be responsible for blocking prophecy or messianic fulfillment. And so, in a moment of great kindness, Jesus heals.

Knowing when to lay down your sword is important. I believe perhaps Jesus is calling us into an even deeper freedom of never wielding one in the first place. How would things change for you if you believed the words spoken long ago, "The LORD will fight for you; you need only to be still" (Exod. 14:14 NIV). God parts the waters, God fights the battles. The battle we must fight is within ourselves.

When we rest assured that the God of the universe—who, as Jesus said, is ready to send twelve legions of angels—will fight for us, we can hold onto our peace and respond in love. Jesus shows us the perfect contrast to Peter's charging into battle. Jesus, having already released himself to the Father's will, walks into the confrontation with peace, truth, and love. Jesus, having already committed himself to the Father's will, responds to the attack with an assurance that God *is* in control, that the arrest and all that follows *must* happen, and so he does not fight. Instead, Jesus offers himself willingly, literally stepping forward into the arrest.

> Jesus, knowing all that was going to happen to him, went out and asked them, "Who is it you want?" "Jesus of Nazareth," they replied. "I am he," Jesus said. (And Judas the traitor was standing there with them.) When

> Jesus said, "I am he," they drew back and fell to the ground. Again he asked them, "Who is it you want?"
> "Jesus of Nazareth," they said. Jesus answered, "I told you that I am he. If you are looking for me, then let these men go." (John 18:4–8 NIV)

The sobering truth is that all this played out *before* Peter started a fight. Imagine, Peter watched all this, watched Jesus step forward and confirm his identity twice, and *then* decided it was a good idea to attack!

Often when we find ourselves in a fight, especially if we are going on the offense, it is likely a result of misreading or misinterpreting Jesus's desire for our lives. I think this is likely what led Peter astray. Just a few hours before in the upper room, Jesus had instructed the disciples to be prepared for things to change. Within a few hours, he would be deemed a criminal and his followers would be in jeopardy. So Jesus, while offering his disciples counsel about how to proceed over those next few days, encourages them to have a place to store money and to have a means of defense—a sword (Luke 22:36–38).

It is possible that those words are ringing in Peter's ears. Having misinterpreted the need for the arrest, death, and resurrection to occur, Peter is far too willing to intercede here. What Christ meant as a means of protection, Peter uses as a means for attack. Don't we do the same thing when we step into a fight we aren't called to?

This misinterpretation, or at least oversight, by Peter is indicative of his continuing disbelief that Jesus was actually going to die and be resurrected. This reality never sank in for the disciples, even to the point that *after* the resurrection, they walked with Jesus on the road to Emmaus and did not recognize him as the risen Christ. I believe this is a danger for us as well. Do we truly believe Christ is who he says he is? If we did, how would that alter our response?

Another problem that arises here is Peter's willingness, eagerness even, to intercede and prevent the suffering that is to come. Peter is determined to save Jesus. The irony of that statement is startling to us. We have the benefit of seeing this situation from an entirely different perspective than Peter did. We have the long-term vision that Peter did not possess in the moment. Instead, he responded based on what he saw and knew in the moment. Peter looked at the situation as it was unfolding in real time with his earthly perspective. This is another trap we easily fall into as well. In the situations we face, the fights we see in front of us, we too are only able to see what happens before us, in real time. To better understand what is happening, we require an eternal vision.

What if some battles are designed to play out without our intervention? If not designed, perhaps permitted to occur. If we are to understand God's will in our lives and the world around us, we must accept that "nothing happens in the universe without his willing or allowing it."[2] When we see something unjust, how do we make sense of it? This must have been a large motivator for Peter as well as he reacted to the injustice he saw before him. Surely we are called to jump in, right?! The answer is, not always. Some injustices, some battles, occur without intervention; yet God uses them for good.

The unjust death of George Floyd, a death not designed by God, was used in this way to bring about something good through the exposing of darkness. His was a tragedy without intervention. But God was determined to make something of it. These are hard and heavy concepts to wrestle with. As we continue to examine God's sovereignty in our lives and the world around us, we must be willing to look at the battles that occur seemingly without

---

[2]Jean Baptiste Saint-Jure, *Trustful Surrender to Divine Providence*, trans. Paul Garvin (Rockford, IL: Tan Books, 1980).

intervention and witness how these are often the times when darkness is unveiled. Yet we can take heart, as Augustine reminds us, knowing God's hands, not ours, are the ones that ultimately bring goodness to this world. "God accomplishes his good will through the evil will of others. . . . in God's hand even evil can bring about good. He would never have permitted evil to occur if he had not, thanks to his perfect goodness, been able to use it."[3]

What if instead of the intervention, God is looking for you to be part of the good that comes after? In the days following George Floyd's death, after having witnessed the darkness of that day on display, there was a new call to confront the racism of our country.

Racism was not a new concept or even a new battle for our family. This is a topic we discuss openly and often. In that last week of May 2020, my soul was screaming. I was ready to jump in and defend. I was horrified, disheartened, and eager to fight. I just didn't know where to go with all my frenetic energy.

The first night of riots in our capital city pressed my husband, Josh, and me to our knees. We live right off the road that connects downtown to suburbia. We heard the sirens racing into the heart of the city. We heard helicopters overhead. It was unnerving—as if the city were coming apart at the seams. There were more sirens—then even more. We prayed a long time that night. Sitting up in bed, clutching each other's hands, and seeking protection for all in the city, for peace and love, for goodness to come out of all this.

Over the next few weeks, we pressed into many hard conversations. We were determined to be voices of hope, love, and reason. We had challenging discussions with many friends. We asked our Black friends to tell us more about their experiences over recent days, months, and years. We listened a lot. We challenged each

---

[3] Augustine quoted in Wilfrid Stinissen, *Into Your Hands, Father: Abandoning Ourselves to the God Who Loves Us*, trans. Clare Marie (San Francisco: Ignatius Press, 2011).

other. We allowed room for growth and new perspectives, both from ourselves and from those around us. And we kept praying.

We asked God to show us whom we were to reach out to. We asked God how we were called to serve. We asked God what we needed to repent of. He answered. We were emboldened in new ways, encouraged in new ways, and commissioned in new ways. I would have been perfectly happy to jump into the fray, ready to duke it out with anyone in my way. Through God's faithful leading, we ended up having exactly the conversations we were designed to have. Through seeking his will first, we knew exactly the way we were called to be part of the answer to the darkness.

I never would have imagined this would look like our entire family showing up on one of the most dangerous blocks in the inner city every week, yet that is precisely what happened. I was ready to jump in, yes, but I was not ready to commit our entire family to over a year of weekly service, yet that is exactly where God wanted to use us. Where I was ready to settle to be another angry voice, God instead invited us to be part of the good that came from the darkness.

Where there could have been unrest in my soul, I had peace because we were obedient. This is huge growth for a challenger-inclined person like me. I can't imagine much good that could have come out of my angst and jumping into every fight, but I have had the joy of seeing what God is doing in that one block in downtown, and it is good.

As we consider what battles are ours to jump in to, we are wise to remember that God is the only one with the battle plan. Throughout history, we see God use imperfect people to bring unexpected good, to expose evil, and to thwart darkness. While we get to participate in this good work, as Esau McCaulley points out in *Reading While Black*, we often have limited discernment about what God is up to. "God brings his judgment against corrupt institutions through *humans* in his own time," McCaulley reminds us.[4] Our prayer, therefore, is to stay in step with God.

May we be prayerful before we raise our sword or wield our tongue. May we recognize that not every fight is ours.

Via Dolorosa Way of Grief

As we follow Jesus from Gethsemane to Golgotha and then to the tomb, take a few moments to sit quietly with him. Similar to the Way of the Cross or Stations of the Cross, we will pause to reflect on the moments and meaning of Good Friday. There is grief in death. But there is also grief in our sin and in our misalignment with God. Before we continue on, we must pause and grieve.

REFLECT

- What do you see in Peter's fight?

- Where are you fighting when you are instead called to lay down your sword?

- As you reflect, ask God to reveal his presence and will. What does he show you?

[4]Esau McCaulley, *Reading While Black: African American Biblical Interpretation as an Exercise in Hope* (Downers Grove, IL: InterVarsity Press, 2020).

CONFESS

- Have you intervened before praying?

- Have you assumed you know what is best?

- Where is there misalignment in your desires, actions, and thoughts?

- Where are you not valuing what Jesus valued?

RECONSIDER

- Letting go of our will and seeking God's will is the way to freedom, beauty, and life.
- The redemptive work begins with letting go of control.
- Take time to pray and affirm this.

CHAPTER THREE

YOU DON'T NEED TO RESPOND

Death of the Rebuttal

Jesus's Trials

Matthew 27:11–14 | Mark 14:60–62, 15:1–5 | Luke 22:66–71, 23:1–3

I am a fierce advocate. And as we already established, I do not naturally shirk away from a fight. Together, these realities create a natural-born arguer. Arguing, especially for what is just, is not necessarily a bad thing. In fact, it can be admirable. The challenge for me is twofold: first, discerning when I am called to enter into an argument, and second, recognizing my unrelenting need to have the last word in the moment.

We have all heard the phrase: you do not need to attend every argument you're invited to. We can easily see the wisdom in it. But what about when the cause is just? What about when truth is on the line?

Truth and justice are hills we may be willing to die on. But what if in our willingness to die on those hills, we miss the opportunity to die on exactly the hill Jesus has for us? For many of us, our need for control is a lot more entangled within our fights for justice than we recognize.

Biblical justice asserts that every human holds *Imago Dei*, the image of God, and therefore is to be treated with dignity as equals. Justice, as we humans tend to use the word, refers to a sense of what is right and wrong, however we define those terms. The challenge comes when we tend to constantly redefine good and evil, particularly based on our own power and positioning.

We often translate that to injustice we may be personally facing. When someone puts words in our mouths. When we are misunderstood, our actions or intentions misconstrued, our reputations tarnished. How do we respond? For many of us, we think the onus is on us to correct the error because it seems intolerable to let a falsehood stand.

Are we looking to win the argument to validate the truth?

Between the hours of approximately 2:00 a.m. and 9:00 a.m., Jesus faces six separate trials. In the first century, there was a tenuous, carefully managed dynamic between the handling and upholding of both Jewish and Roman law. Both systems were upheld and enforced simultaneously, and often, very much entangled. So much so that Jews, upon being sentenced by the Sanhedrin for breaking Jewish law, would be turned over to the Romans for judgment and punishment if they could find, or create, proof that Roman law was also broken.

As we know, from Gethsemane, Jesus is arrested by the high priests, and that is when his trials begin. First, Jesus faces Annas, the former high priest (John 18:12–14); then Caiaphas, the current high priest (Matt. 26:57–68); and then the Sanhedrin, the governing council and court, as a whole (Matt. 27:1–2; Luke 22:63–71).

Jesus is charged with blasphemy and false prophecy. The trials were a sham. The Jewish leaders were blatantly breaking their own rules in an effort to get a charge that would stick. Matthew 26:59–61 gives us a glimpse into this:

> The chief priests and the whole Sanhedrin were looking for false testimony against Jesus so that they could put him to death, but they could not find any, even though many false witnesses came forward. Finally, two who came forward stated, "This man said, 'I can destroy the temple of God and rebuild it in three days.'"

The Sanhedrin, by gathering in the predawn hours, were already outside their own law.[1] The Sanhedrin, having already established their end goal as Jesus's death, were simply looking for anyone willing to testify against him so that they could accomplish their goal. But they could not find anyone. Even though plenty of false witnesses came forward, they were not able to piece together a testimony of his heresy or false prophecy. Under the law, the Sanhedrin heard each testimony separately, and any conflicting testimony was deemed unacceptable. All they could find were two individuals willing to quote Jesus as saying he would destroy and raise the temple again in three days as we read in Matthew 26:61. This quote was taken completely out of context. In fact, John specifically articulated that when Jesus spoke those words, he was not being literal. In response to Jesus saying, "Destroy this temple, and I will raise it up in three days" (John 2:19), John said, "But he was speaking about the temple of his body" (v. 21). Jesus never threatened to destroy the actual temple. This was not valid grounds for a conviction.

---

[1] This was one of many ways in which the Sanhedrin were acting outside of its governing principles, thus making the trials illegitimate. Other offenses included having a trial during a feast, lack of individual voting on conviction by members of the Sanhedrin, lack of representation for the accused, and asking self-incriminating questions of the accused.

Even still, each religious trial convicted him and sent him on to the next trial in rapid order—first Annas, then Caiaphas, and then finally the Sanhedrin. "Then the high priest stood up before them all and questioned Jesus, 'Don't you have an answer to what these men are testifying against you?' But he kept silent and did not answer" (Mark 14:60–61).

While Jesus is being accused of false prophecy by the desperate Sanhedrin, just outside, at the same exact time, Peter is denying the Lord three times and thus fulfilling prophecy from the night before (Luke 22:54–62). The simultaneous trial against Jesus while Scripture is being fulfilled is shocking. How blind we can be to what God is doing, even when it happens right before our eyes.

Meanwhile, the Sanhedrin are desperate for a charge that will stick to Jesus to justify his death. The accusation against Jesus for being the Messiah, the Son of God, originated from an understanding that the Messiah would come to crush Rome and establish himself as an earthly king. Jesus never confessed to being the Messiah in front of the Sanhedrin. What he did do was simply turn the words of the Sanhedrin back to themselves. They asked, "Are you, then, the Son of God?" And he responded, "You say that I am" (Luke 22:70).

It was as if Jesus was acknowledging that their understanding of who the Messiah would be and how he would unseat Rome, and them, from power had already been decided. The Sanhedrin had already decided the outcome of this decision before Jesus was arrested. The trial and accusations, the asking for a defense, were simply a pretense to add legitimacy to this totally illegitimate affair. In such a way, here Jesus is just restating the Sanhedrin's opinion back to them. And this opinion, their own, was all that the Sanhedrin needed to turn Jesus over to the even bigger power of the day—the Romans.

After the religious leaders found Jesus guilty, he was then turned over to the Romans. This was customary, as the Messiah, a king, would be a threat to Rome and therefore the Sanhedrin could move Jesus's case along to the governmental powers, the powers that held the authority to execute, without losing face.

The Roman trials were with Governor Pilate, then to Herod Antipas, and then back to Pilate. Remember, all these trials were finished by 9:00 a.m. Things were happening very quickly. Along with a fast progression came a whole new list of accusations.

"Then their whole assembly rose up and brought him before Pilate. They began to accuse him, saying, 'We found this man misleading our nation, opposing payment of taxes to Caesar, and saying that he himself is the Messiah, a king'" (Luke 23:1–2). Thus the Sanhedrin laid out three reasons why Pilate should convict Jesus: misleading Israel, opposing payment of taxes to Rome, and asserting he was a king in conflict with Roman authority. Not one of these accusations could stand, as they were all false and easily disproved.

Jesus was someone Rome had been keeping an eye on for a while. They were already familiar with his teachings. Even Rome could attest that his teachings were not aimed at misleading Israel. Regarding the payment of taxes, the Sanhedrin had themselves established Jesus's stance, which was contradictory to the charge. They had attempted to publicly corner Jesus on this topic, and Jesus clearly had demonstrated to be in favor of paying taxes: "Give to Caesar the things that are Caesar's" (Luke 20:20–26). Including this accusation simply demonstrates the Sanhedrin's desperation and willingness to manufacture "facts" as a way to indict Jesus. Lastly, the charge of his being a king is also something Rome would have been monitoring closely. Jesus was always very careful to assert and confirm that his kingdom was *not* of this earth, and therefore not a threat to Rome. And here is the important part: Pilate knew all this.

Pilate was in a no-win situation, and he knew that too.

Upon realizing Jesus was a Galilean, Pilate thought he had found his way out of the mess by passing Jesus on to Herod Antipas, who held the jurisdiction for Galilee. Pilate was hopeful he could send this down to the local authorities and thus de-escalate the trial out of his jurisdiction. Both Herod and Pilate were in Jerusalem, as the festival of Passover was happening, and they were required to "keep an eye on things." This is important to note because had the events taken place some other week, none of the pieces would have been in play to bring about the events of this day.

What follows is a fascinating scene in which Herod, thrilled to finally meet the miracle man everyone had been talking about, is eager to see a miracle performed. Jesus does not comply. In fact, he once again stays silent (Luke 23:9). The chief priests and scribes are present for this interaction and are reeling. There is frustration and screaming on their part. Herod loses his temper, mocks Jesus, and then sends him back to Pilate.

Pilate is not at all pleased to have this problem back in his lap. He is frustrated at the trials he can clearly see are not warranted:

> Pilate called together the chief priests, the leaders, and the people, and said to them, "You have brought me this man as one who misleads the people. But in fact, after examining him in your presence, I have found no grounds to charge this man with those things you accuse him of. Neither has Herod, because he sent him back to us. Clearly, he has done nothing to deserve death." (Luke 23:13–15)

Thus ends the final three trials. This time, from the government. And each one resulted in an acquittal. And yet we know that death was indeed imminent. As the trials conclude, Pilate is left to decide what happens next. There are the screaming religious leaders, the frustrated government leaders. Most shocking of all, there was this: "But Jesus still did not answer, and so Pilate was amazed" (Mark 15:5).

The trials of Jesus leave me with so many questions. Was this simply a way to get to the cross? Are we called to be silent as well? What about justice? Why do we feel it is necessary to defend ourselves?

What I do know is that we are not called to be silent in matters of injustice toward others. There is total clarity about that as we see Jesus intercede for the marginalized, the forgotten. He specifically calls us to serve those who are most often not seen or served. Therefore, we must not misunderstand his silence before those who tried him as complacency. This is a specific call to reconsider how we argumentatively defend ourselves. It is *not* a call to stay silent when we see any of the above happening to others. Jesus is clear on this. The Bible is clear on this. We must speak up for the voiceless.

It is also easy to misinterpret Jesus's silence as an indication that he thinks nothing of himself, a radical humility that garners an inability to defend oneself. While this type of humility is certainly present, I think there is something more for us as well. I believe we are called to see a man so deeply rooted in who he is and whose he is that the words of man have no power.

This changes everything.

The trials are an excellent example to us of how fickle people can be. Innocence and guilt were turned upside down in those early morning hours of Good Friday. The benchmark for truth must come from God and God alone. Jesus knew that, and it is from that deep understanding that he stands silent in front of the Sanhedrin and the governors as they argue and angle to convince themselves of their own versions of reality.

Silence or screaming does not change the truth.

There was no just outcome or justice to be found that morning, outside of God himself. If Jesus, the brilliant orator and wordsmith, were to get in the fray with any of the parties coming at him, he would have validated them as worthy adversaries. Which they certainly were not. They were not seeking truth nor justice.

When we recognize that God is the only arbiter of truth, the issue of speaking up on our behalf changes from one of justice and right to one of peace. Your peace. In both Mark 14:61 and Matthew 26:63, we read about how Jesus "kept silent." The Greek word used here is *siōpaō*. The word literally means "to hold one's peace." This word *siōpaō* evokes an involuntary response—I would argue, a response to God. It is the same word used to describe Zechariah as he exited the temple (Luke 1:22), as well as the same word uttered by Jesus as he calmed the seas (Luke 8:24).

How often in our quest to justify, correct, or communicate our words, position, or stance do we sacrifice the peace available to us? When we remember who we are and whose we are, we can leave our reputation in Christ's hands. In so doing, we are able to more fully hold our peace and to grow our faith. Jim Wilder, in his book *Renovated*, quotes the spiritual formation master Dallas Willard as saying, "to be able to not engage in image management is a sign of great faith. To resign your image to God and let Him take control of it, so you don't need to manage it, is a great step forward in spiritual life."[2]

When I look at these trials, I see the confidence of truth rooted in God and the peace that is available to us as we may face persecution, misrepresentation, defamation, and slander.

As we put this into practice, we will likely encounter the reactions of both the Sanhedrin and the governors for ourselves. Our

---

[2]Jim Wilder, *Renovated: God, Dallas Willard, and the Church That Transforms* (Colorado Springs, CO: NavPress, 2020).

silence, where there once was rebuttal, will likely draw confusion. Beyond that, we can expect to face screaming, literally and figuratively. If those who plot against us are truly looking for a fight and we do not offer ourselves as a contestant, this will quite likely enrage them. Just as we see the Sanhedrin spin into chaos, that too may be what we face. Our silence and holding our peace will ultimately, however, confuse and befuddle. To hold silent when an argument is expected, to disengage rather than defend, may be the loudest example of Jesus our accusers ever experience. May our willingness to stand in the truth of God as a sufficient defender of truth be a way to show them God himself. And with that, may they, just as Pilate was, be amazed.

Via Dolorosa Way of Grief

As we follow Jesus from Gethsemane to Golgotha and then to the tomb take a few moments to sit quietly with him. Similar to the Way of the Cross or Stations of the Cross we will pause to reflect on the moments and meaning of Good Friday. There is grief in death. There is also grief in our sin and in our misalignment with God. Before we continue on we must pause and grieve.

REFLECT

- What do you see as you watch Jesus remain silent?

- Have you seen truth cast aside in your own life?

- As you reflect, ask God to reveal his presence and will. What does he show you?

CONFESS

- Have you defended yourself against false claims?
- Do you value man's opinion over God's?
- Where is there misalignment in your desires, actions, and thoughts?
- Where are you not valuing what Jesus valued?

RECONSIDER

- Letting go of our will and seeking God's will is the way to freedom, beauty, and life.
- The redemptive work begins with letting go of control.
- Take time to pray and affirm this.

PART TWO

Not All Letting Go Is Good

While we are called to let go of control, we can experience havoc and destruction in our lives if we let go of the wrong things. We see them in close succession on Good Friday with the death of hope, death of the compassionate crowd, and death of reason. Fortunately, we are not called to cast aside hope, compassion, or reason to flourish with God. In fact, we will see how the opposite is true.

CHAPTER FOUR

WHEN ALL SEEMS LOST

Death of Hope

Judas

Matt. 27:3–10

When Jesus announced to the disciples at the Last Supper that one of them would betray him, it was shocking. When you closely read each Gospel account, you realize: no one knew who it would be. The response from the group wasn't, "Oh, of course it's going to be Judas." Instead, they asked, *Who? Could it be me? Could it be you?*

Don't miss this.

Judas wasn't the obvious betrayer because there was no obvious betrayer. He wasn't the only one hanging on by a thread—although as you read the text you realize there was a sense that perhaps they all were.

There is far more relatability in Judas than we imagine. When we only consider him as "the betrayer," we keep him as an outsider. When we set him aside as not just the one who ultimately betrayed Jesus but as the only one capable of this, we alienate him in a way that makes us more comfortable and offers more distance. However, I believe there is much to learn when we see the bigger picture of Judas. His, as the scripture shows, is a story of hope and hopelessness, of being used and abused, of feeling like there was nowhere to go in pain and poor decisions.

> Then Judas, his betrayer, seeing that Jesus had been condemned, was full of remorse and returned the thirty pieces of silver to the chief priests and elders. "I have sinned by betraying innocent blood," he said. "What's that to us?" they said. "See to it yourself!" So he threw the silver into the temple and departed. Then he went and hanged himself. The chief priests took the silver and said, "It's not permitted to put it into the temple treasury, since it is blood money." They conferred together and bought the potter's field with it as a burial place for foreigners. Therefore that field has been called "Field of Blood" to this day. Then what was spoken through the prophet Jeremiah was fulfilled: They took the thirty pieces of silver, the price of him whose price was set by the Israelites, and they gave them for the potter's field, as the Lord directed me. (Matt. 27:3–10)

Have you ever considered what was happening inside Judas on the day he decided to betray Jesus? When we think of Judas, there is no other right response than the deepest empathy. The finger-pointing, the shame, the scapegoating—there is no place for any of it. To understand how things played out for Judas on Good Friday, I think it is wise to first consider how he got into the position in the first place. Luke 22:2–3 describes the factors Judas was struggling against. "The chief priests and the scribes were looking for a way to put him to death, because they were afraid of the people. Then

Satan entered Judas, called Iscariot, who was numbered among the Twelve."

It was the religious leaders who were seeking a way to eliminate Jesus, not Judas. And Satan? Well, Satan recognized a great opportunity to seize and did so. It is under that power that Judas proceeded, and it was that power, the power of Satan, the leaders responded to with delight.

The weight of this never really hit me until I listened to a song[1] from Judas's perspective. In the song he spoke of being a puppet and not knowing how to stop what was happening. It was as if he was simply a passenger being pulled along.

I've been there. Have you?

A bad decision, a momentary loss of judgment, can easily lead you down a path that you had no intention of taking. Satan loves this and will use this to keep you deeper in a pit, further away from Jesus. Then you look around and realize you are lost.

This is where we find Judas in the very early hours of that Friday morning.

As Judas became aware that the Sanhedrin had Jesus in their grasp, he realized that Jesus was condemned. Judas's death was said to take place in the middle of the trials as Jesus was being bounced around from Pilate to Herod and back again. Judas thought he knew the end of the story. In despair, he believed all was lost. What Judas did not realize was that the story was not yet concluded. He was in the middle of something, but through the lens of his remorse and despondency, he believed it to be the conclusion.

Judas mistook the middle for the end.

The middle of anything is a messy place, even the middle of a miracle. This is where we are called to spend most of our time.

---

[1]Gabriel Brown, Chase Crandell, and Giovanni Beatty, "Lost Cause," by Anna Miriam Brown, Apple Music, track 25 on *His Story the Musical* (Original Cast Recording), Thinking Tree LLC, 2019.

The middle finds us aware of a need not yet realized. The middle is where there is not yet a cure, not yet restoration. When we hold on to hope, the middle is where we can say, "Not done yet."

However, when we confuse the middle for the end, everything shifts. If we perceive our middle to be the end of the story, we experience the messy middle "not yet" very differently. It is in this disconnect where we lose perspective, lose connection, and lose hope. We can often proclaim a finality to something that was never meant to be forever—especially when we are lost. That misjudgment of calling the middle the end is what leads us to a place of despair. In our disorientation, we proclaim that all seems lost.

Through a miraculous reconsideration, Judas does decide to do something in the face of his despair. He acts. He repents and retracts. Judas returns the money to the leadership and confesses his wrongdoing. Matthew 27:3–4 says, "Judas . . . was full of remorse and returned the thirty pieces of silver to the chief priests and elders. 'I have sinned by betraying innocent blood,' he said."

Why do we not see this as the heroic, humble act it truly is? He returns and confesses. I have to believe God was rejoicing in this moment as Judas came home to the temple, his church, to try again. Even still, it is the response of humans to this action that is perhaps the most tragic.

The leadership scoffs. They minimize the magnitude of Judas's regret. And then, they isolate him. It is a shocking response to a person in pain. "Not my problem."

I wish I could say this isn't a response we can relate to today. Sadly, I imagine we can relate to both sides of that response. Have you felt the sting of rejection as you struggled? Have you had a friend or mentor or leader shrug you off, minimize what you are going through, perhaps even with a cruel word thrown in to make you feel small? It stings. And it is the kind of sting that lasts. If you have ever conjured up enough bravery to confess a hurt or problem only to have it be met with belittlement or brushed aside, then you know. If you are in a place of repentance, confession, and retracting your past, you are rightly longing to be seen in your pain, in your sorrow, in your despair.

But, then again, how often do we, in an attempt to regain comfort, minimize someone else's suffering or repentance? It may not be as blatant as "What's it to me?!" but we can easily paint a sunny picture where someone is experiencing darkness. We may minimize their pain by focusing on the bright side without having sat with them, right where they are. Even more so, we may brush aside the pain they are feeling as something that we don't need to own, and therefore, in distancing ourselves from them, either literally or figuratively, we send a clear message: "That's your problem, not mine."

A person struggling *must* be met with a personal response. To respond in such a way that communicates they are seen, their pain matters, and their problems are worthy of our full attention is critical. For the one brave enough to say "help me," there is nothing more powerful than hearing that "me" turned into a "we." We will get through this. We will get help. We will pray. When we personally step into another's pain, when we come alongside them, hope is immediately infused into the situation.

It is only after being cast aside without care that we see Judas respond in, perhaps, anger and then commit suicide. The desperation powerful enough to drive him to this comes only after he has been scoffed at, isolated, and belittled.

This is heartbreaking. What if it wasn't his regret that led him to suicide? What if it was the deep loneliness he felt after being admonished by the priests? What if it was the sense that there was nowhere left to go? For Judas, in that moment, what if the only options he saw were death for the crime of false testimony or suicide?

The story of Judas has been manipulated to be a story of what happens when we turn our back on Jesus. I believe we have gotten that completely wrong. When I read the Scripture, I see a story of what happens when a repentant person, after having gone astray, is denied space to turn around. What has been turned into a terrifying story for one who has gone off course is *actually* a story of warning for those receiving the hopeless-but-seeking, those who are repentant yet unsure.

How do we receive the one who is lost? Hurt? Hopeless?

As Judas commits suicide, the priests are busy sorting out what to do with the money he left. They devise a way to use the money yet not hold themselves in association with it, thus buying what is called the potter's field. Today we understand that this is a fulfillment of the prophecy foretold in Zechariah 11:12–13.[2] This was their focus as Judas came, overtaken by remorse. The leaders were focused on clearing themselves from any wrongdoing and figuring out where to put the blood money so that it had the least effect on their leadership.

The void of earnest, biblical church leadership we see in the use and abuse of Judas is chilling. The way a leader cares for you will greatly determine your view of the church, your faith, your worth. I believe in this account of hopelessness, the role of the church leadership cannot be overstated.

What I see when I reflect on this entire account is a person who is scared, exhausted, distraught, and unsure. I see a person who was manipulated and used by those in power and then left shame-filled and alone in his confusion and hopelessness.

Alone is exactly where the enemy would have us sit.

---

[2]The original Scripture of Matthew 27:9 refers to the prophet Jeremiah. It is widely held that Matthew was referring to the book of the Prophets, which contained the prophetic writings the current Bible breaks up into smaller books, including Zechariah.

If you relate to any of the descriptions of Judas, know this: in the middle of all the confusion and hopelessness, in the middle of any bad decision or unsure future, Jesus loves you more than anyone ever will. As Judas was in the middle of the betrayal, as he realized the consequences of his actions, as he was turned away by the priests and left alone in his mess, Jesus was buying his freedom through his very own death. And he has done the same for you. Even in the middle of the uncertainty, the turning around, the confusion, the feeling of being lost. He is all the hope you need and the only hope you need.

Feeling hopeless will crush you. It will take your life away. We have all been touched, personally, by suicide and suicide prevention efforts. Hope is the beginning and the end of it all. We were not made to live without it.

The first time I was face-to-face with suicide was sometime during my senior year of high school. I attended the funeral of a college-aged boy who had taken his life. I didn't know him or his family—I was there to represent an organization we had in common. I had never heard wailing at a wake like I heard that day. I can still hear the cries of his sister and mother some twenty-five years later. It haunts me. This was the first of many interactions with suicide or suicide ideation.

There is a suicide crisis facing our world right now. Even before we faced eighteen months of varying degrees of isolation during the COVID-19 pandemic, there were rampant numbers of suicide and suicide ideation. And then, during the first six months of 2020, the calls to suicide hotlines increased by 800 percent.[3] In other words, we are surrounded by people barely holding on. Or perhaps we are ourselves experiencing that terrible sensation of

[3] J. Matthew Sleeth, *Hope Always: How to Be a Force for Life in a Culture of Suicide* (Carol Stream, IL: Tyndale House, 2021), 30.

hope slipping through our fingers. The enemy thrives in this place where hope runs thin, but he does not get to have the final say. The lies of Satan will point to death, and that is why we must cling to Jesus and point to hope, the hope that can only be found in the one who loves you even while you are at your darkest, deepest place, when you are still in the middle of the story.

For those responding to the lost, or the ones who believe hope is dead for them, may we remember that we can hold hope for them. We can be sure about the hope we hold and that it is strong enough to hold for someone else as well. While we do that, we can bear witness to the middle of their story. We can sit in the pain of the middle and be the one to remind them we do not need to mistake the middle for the end.

It's not that we can fix it, but we can stay beside them, stand in the gap, bear witness, and hold on to hope for them when it keeps slipping through their fingers. Bearing witness, rather than brushing aside, and believing our friends or family when they are struggling is perhaps the greatest gift we can offer them as they find their way back to hope.

And sometimes, every once in a while, we get to sit alongside them right smack dab in the middle of a miracle, the realization that all is not lost. It's not that we have much to do with the solution, but we can stay beside them, being a recordkeeper of the miracle, call it what it is, and hand them back their hope. Dr. Matthew Sleeth calls this the Ministry of Presence.[4] I am grateful for each time I get to do both—sit in the struggle and sit in the miracle.

For all of us, may we know deep within our souls that there is no decision or choice we cannot turn back from. The enemy may call to us; all may seem lost or perhaps too far gone. But this miracle is true: there is no such thing as too far gone in the kingdom of

---

[4] Sleeth, *Hope Always*, 159–60.

God. What was true for Judas is true of us today—we are not called to let go of hope. May we hold tight to the hope found in Jesus and all he did on Good Friday. May we, if we are the ones receiving the hopeless, be a place of comfort as we hold hope on their behalf and tenderly hand it back to them as we say, "Don't let go."

Via Dolorosa Way of Grief

As we follow Jesus from Gethsemane to Golgotha and then to the tomb, take a few moments to sit quietly with him. Similar to the Way of the Cross or Stations of the Cross, we will pause to reflect on the moments and meaning of Good Friday. There is grief in death. But there is also grief in our sin and in our misalignment with God. Before we continue on, we must pause and grieve.

REFLECT

- What new things are you considering about Judas?
- What is the role of hope?
- As you reflect, ask God to reveal his presence and will. What does he show you?

CONFESS

- Have you received the hopeless well?

- Have you mistaken the middle for the end of the miracle?

- Where is there misalignment in your desires, actions, and thoughts?

- Where are you not valuing what Jesus valued?

RECONSIDER

- Letting go of our will and seeking God's will is the way to freedom, beauty, and life.
- The redemptive work begins with letting go of control.
- Take time to pray and affirm this.

CHAPTER FIVE

CROWD CONTROL

Death of the Compassionate Crowd

Jesus in Front of the Crowd

Matthew 27:17–20 | Mark 15:11 | Luke 23:22–23 | John 19:15–16

Throughout Jesus's earthly ministry, we often see a crowd around him. The Gospels mention "the crowd" at least one hundred times. It was this gathering crowd that represented the biggest threat to the existing religious power structure of the Pharisees and Sadducees. With great precision and tactical skill, it was a crowd that religious power structure used to ultimately condemn Jesus.

The scene in front of Pilate's judgment seat in those early morning hours is a reminder that every crowd has a leader, and the character and tone of that leader can change everything. It is still quite early in the morning. News is just beginning to spread about Jesus's arrest. The crowds gathered here are likely the locals of Jerusalem, not the pilgrims who came into the city for Passover and not likely Jesus's followers. In other words, the crowd gathering is made up of curious onlookers and the ones who study and learn under the Pharisees and Sadducees of the city.

The crowd we see the morning of Good Friday stands in stark contrast to the crowds we saw gathered around Jesus. This is because the leadership we see in the Pharisees stands in stark contrast to the leadership we see demonstrated by Jesus himself. Let's take a closer look.

The crowds that gathered around Jesus are reflective of who he was as a leader. They were marked by teaching, healing, generosity, humility, and faith. We see this in the accounts of feeding the five thousand, lowering a friend through a hole in the roof to ensure his access to healing, and listening to the rabbi teach for hours throughout the day. We see compassion and care, abundance and freedom.

Jesus seemed to be aware of two things as he led these crowds: their access to him and his own spiritual health. This is the mark of healthy leadership. As news spread of Jesus's healings and teachings, the crowds began to grow and gather around him and the disciples. Jesus was never accepting of the crowd blocking the way to him. We see several instances where someone was clamoring to get to Jesus—children, the sick, the desperate—and often a disciple would step in and try to control access to Jesus. But Jesus interceded. He would tell the disciples, "Let them come to me" (Matt. 19:14). Jesus was intent on granting access to the healing and mercy and grace that only he could provide. No crowd could thwart it.

My favorite example of this is found in Jesus's interactions with Zacchaeus, the tree-climbing tax collector:

> He entered Jericho and was passing through. And behold, there was a man named Zacchaeus. He was a chief tax collector and was rich. And he was seeking to

> see who Jesus was, but on account of the crowd he could not, because he was small in stature. So he ran on ahead and climbed up into a sycamore tree to see him, for he was about to pass that way. And when Jesus came to the place, he looked up and said to him, "Zacchaeus, hurry and come down, for I must stay at your house today." So he hurried and came down and received him joyfully. (Luke 19:1–6 ESV)

It wasn't until I started meditating on my role in today's crowds that I noticed verse three—it stopped me dead in my tracks. "And he was seeking to see who Jesus was, but on account of the crowd he could not, because he was small in stature." Zacchaeus was *seeking Jesus*, and the *crowd* was the reason why he could not see who Jesus was. I believe this is far more than a literal statement on crowd control and lines of sight.[1] I believe there is a tremendously important lesson for us here. The nature, perhaps even the existence, of the crowd was preventing someone looking for Jesus to be able to find him.

But once again, Jesus did not allow the crowd to block or obstruct the way to him. Jesus went right up to Zacchaeus and interceded. And as we continue to read in Luke, Jesus even went to Zacchaeus's home and changed his whole life. Freedom was found.

Jesus was also focused on his own spiritual health. The crowds were exhausting, and in several passages of Scripture, when the crowds thronged to Jesus, we see him step away. Jesus was regularly found retreating to the water or to a quiet place alone to pray. Jesus was intent on maintaining his own time alone, with the Father, so that he could refresh and refuel for the crowds.

---

[1]I also believe the use of stature, *hēlikia* in Greek, is used here to demonstrate immaturity more so than height. Thus the literal reading of this verse becomes even more problematic. Zacchaeus wasn't small of stature; he was a not-yet-mature man, seeking and yearning to know more about Jesus.

As the news about Jesus spread, large crowds would come together to hear him and to be healed from their sicknesses. Yet Jesus often withdrew to deserted places and prayed (Luke 5:15–16).

Jesus didn't use his platform to gain notoriety or fame. The crowds did not confirm who he was or serve as a means to validate his sense of self. Jesus showed up to the crowds to seek and to save (Luke 19:10). Jesus went to the crowds to serve, and then when he was depleted, he went back to the quiet place to refill his own soul by spending time with his Father in prayer.

The word used to describe these quiet places is the Greek word *erēmos*. It is a fascinating term. *Erēmos* is the word used to describe the wilderness of Jesus's forty days, where he went in preparation for the beginning of his ministry and battled Satan. It is the word used to describe the solitary, lonely, desolate, uninhabited places we find John the Baptist. It is the word used to describe the place where Jesus would go to pray. It is the word used to describe the place he and the disciples would go to rest. *Erēmos* is a quiet place to find renewal in God the Father.

As a ministry leader, I am humbled when I consider how critical *erēmos* was to Jesus. It appears there is no other way to lead a crowd well than to be seeking *erēmos* for yourself consistently. When we stop and spend time with God, seeking rest and renewal in him, seeking a place to pray and cry out and to be reminded of who we are, we can show up to a crowd and seek no approval from them. If, instead, we see the crowd as our validation, our filling up, we will lead them astray and forsake our very souls at the same time.

This is what we see play out as the Pharisees take control of the crowd on Good Friday. We see the leaders grasping for control, willing to forsake even God himself, in an effort to cling to their own power. The crowd of people had presumably gathered to see what prisoner would be released by Pilate, per tradition, for Passover.

This tradition was long-standing, even before Roman rule, and served as a means of demonstrating the Romans' acknowledgment of the sovereignty of the Jews. During the Roman era, this also served as a token of assurance to the masses gathered in Jerusalem for Passover that the government would not interfere with the holiday.[2] The Passover tradition of releasing the prisoner is something we will get into in more detail in the following chapter. For now, it is important to note that this tradition was long-standing; thus, both the Pharisees and Pilate were aware of it and used their knowledge to help them each achieve their own end.

Here's what happened:

> So when they had gathered together, Pilate said to them, "Who is it you want me to release for you—Barabbas, or Jesus who is called Christ?" For he knew it was because of envy that they had handed him over. . . . The chief priests and the elders, however, persuaded the crowds to ask for Barabbas and to execute Jesus. (Matt. 27:17–18, 20)

> But the chief priests stirred up the crowd so that he would release Barabbas to them instead. (Mark 15:11)

> A third time he said to them, "Why? What has this man done wrong? I have found in him no grounds for the death penalty. Therefore, I will have him whipped and then release him." But they kept up the pressure, demanding with loud voices that he be crucified, and their voices won out. (Luke 23:22–23)

The Pharisees manipulated the crowd to do their bidding. The choice of which prisoner to release was presented not to the

---

[2]Charles B. Chavel, "The Releasing of a Prisoner on the Eve of Passover in Ancient Jerusalem," *Journal of Biblical Literature* 60, no. 3 (1941): 273–78.

Pharisees alone but to the crowd. I wonder how committed this crowd was to the release of either prisoner? Was Jesus anything to them, besides another troublemaker? Surely, some of his followers had made their way to the judgment seat by then. It seems there must have been some mixed responses at first, because there was some persuading going on: "The chief priests and the elders, however, persuaded the crowds to ask for Barabbas and to execute Jesus" (Matt. 27:20).

Scripture describes the scene in graphic detail. A mob had assembled, and while people waited, the loud voices of the religious leaders stirred them up. Psychologists call this mob mentality, or deindividuation—it is the process by which the presence of other people affects how an individual responds. Deindividuation allows a singular loud voice to control a large group of people.[3] What we see here is a mob being used to advance the power of a select few individuals. I don't believe the mob even realized they were being used—they simply showed up to see who would be released and were then thrust into something much bigger, unbeknownst to themselves.

The Pharisees were relentless. They whipped the crowd into a near riot to assert their power. Luke tells us they "kept up the pressure" (23:23). This was not a mob swept up in a self-created frenzy. This was a crowd being controlled and manipulated.

This is a cautionary tale about grasping for power. As the crowd chanted "Crucify him!," the Pharisees declared their allegiance as well, in John 19:15:

> But they shouted, "Take him away! Take him away!
> Crucify him!"

---

[3]Groupthink is similar but different, and is demonstrated when an individual willingly gives up their self-interest in favor of what is best for the group. That is not what we see in the crowd on Good Friday.

"Shall I crucify your king?" Pilate asked.

"We have no king but Caesar," the chief priests answered.

Imagine, as they fought and clung to their power, the Pharisees began to boast about forsaking God. They were so disillusioned they cried out, in front of the King of Kings himself, that they held allegiance to no one other than the Roman government. Imagine being so disconnected. Imagine willfully leading so many astray.

Of course, in our own lives, we see this far too often. We see crowds throng to social media under the headship of one influencer or another—a leader—who turns to the crowd to validate their own power and influence. It's toxic. And, just like Good Friday, it all ends in destruction. The white-knuckle grasp on power leads to death.

For a little over ten years, I worked in retail. I loved it. I was, as my boss would often remind me, "A natural-born retailer." This was most evident on that uniquely American pseudo-holiday, Black Friday. Of all the things I missed when I stepped away from retail, the thrill of Black Friday was at the top of the list. Every year on Black Friday, I would open the store—in the early 2000s, this meant an arrival of 5:00 a.m. for a 6:00 a.m. open. The store would be stuffed and ready, each table overfilled with wool sweaters at shockingly low prices, round racks overhung with the T-shirts marked down to the lowest price imaginable.

Throughout the day, we would stock and restock as items flew off the shelves and out the door. I can remember catching the eye of my coworker, a dear friend, across the store as he was hauling anything out from the stockroom he could find to sell. As quickly as we could get items out, they would be gone. The shoppers were ready to hunt, and our job was to keep the machine filled. It was chaotic and crazy and thrilling. At some point along the way, we realized we were controlling the crowd. Whatever we placed before them was scooped up. We were pulling out items that had not been sold in years. But in the heat of the moment, in the height of the frenetic energy that is Black Friday, we could sell anything—no matter the style, the price, the value. They had bought into the hype of the day and were completely swept up in the crowd of consumerism.

Was this particular crowd destructive? No. But I can say that we were not stewarding that crowd well. We were serving ourselves, or more accurately, the company we worked for. We were giddy with the power we had over the shoppers and, more than anything, were in disbelief that the shopping crowd was going along with it. Years later, I finally made a shift to a genuine perspective of service. But on that day, and many other Black Fridays, it was about riding the energy wave of the crowd and, sadly, using that energy for our own gain.

Hear me, not all crowds are bad. Not all crowds lead to destruction. It depends entirely on the stewardship of the crowd, the leadership. As I look around at the crowds I belong to today, I ask myself, does this crowd create a clear path to Jesus? What are the leaders, or I as the leader, doing to ensure the crowd is one of service and generosity?

As a founder of a growing ministry, I was hesitant to truly step into my role as leader. As our event numbers began to grow, as we were serving more and more women, our response as cofounders was to shirk back as the face of the ministry. We did not want followers, and yet hundreds of women were going where we led them. It was terrifying. I was finally able to step into the calling of this ministry when I realized that if we kept Jesus as the focus and the destination, then we could lead others not to us but to him. *This* was what I wanted to do with a crowd. If I chased after Jesus hard, whoever might be coming along next to me, or even behind me, would also be chasing him. Together, we would grow closer to Jesus and more likely reflect him. Our ministry thrives because we are constantly asking each other if we are in step with Jesus or blocking him. We make sure he is the hero of every story we tell. We make sure everyone sees a clear path to Jesus. A crowd that has one goal: Jesus. I would have been so sad to have missed being part of such a thing.

We are all leaders, just as we all are members of various crowds. The question is what are we doing with that? Are we grasping for power? Seeking control over a mob, or perhaps losing our soul accumulating a throng with no real plan for how to steward them well? Or are we willing to let go of our grasp for our own power, clear the path to Jesus, and then fill ourselves back up with the true power that comes from spending time with God in the quiet places? May we steward our crowds well and may we be mindful of the crowds we get swept up in.

Via Dolorosa Way of Grief

As we follow Jesus from Gethsemane to Golgotha and then to the tomb, take a few moments to sit quietly with him. Similar to the Way of the Cross or Stations of the Cross, we will pause to reflect on the moments and meaning of Good Friday. There is grief in death. But there is also grief in our sin and in our misalignment with God. Before we continue on, we must pause and grieve.

REFLECT

- What is your involvement with the crowd?

- Are you leading a crowd?

- As you reflect, ask God to reveal his presence and will. What does he show you?

CONFESS

- Does your involvement in a crowd block the way for others to see Jesus?

- Does your attachment to a crowd have more to do with personal power or position?

- Where is there misalignment in your desires, actions, and thoughts?

- Where are you not valuing what Jesus valued?

RECONSIDER

- Letting go of our will and seeking God's will is the way to freedom, beauty, and life.
- The redemptive work begins with letting go of control.
- Take time to pray and affirm this.

CHAPTER SIX

SEEKING TRUTH

Death of Reason

Jesus Condemned to Crucifixion

Matthew 27:15–26 | Mark 15:6–15 | Luke 23:13–25 | John 18:38–40, 19:12–16

We have examined what happens to a crowd when the leaders are corrupt, when we abandon compassion and allow manipulation to take its place. Now, we are going to look closely at Pilate and see what happened with him—the one who acknowledged Jesus's innocence but still condemned him to be crucified.

After the Pharisees had successfully stirred up the crowd at Jesus's trial, we see his accusers and the crowd let go of all reason and the willingness to stand up for truth. Ultimately, the decision of whom to release must be made by Pilate.

Here stand Jesus and Barabbas. Jesus, the one whom Pilate could not condemn, the one who had been cleared of all Roman charges. Barabbas, guilty of murder during a rebellion, condemned to death row in a Roman prison. The name Barabbas translates to "Son of Father." Imagine that. The actual Son of God the Father, a sinless perfect man, standing next to a convicted murderer with the name Son of Father (Bar Abbas). It was quite literally the truest version of that name next to an imitation. One of them would be set free by Pilate.

Mark describes the heartbreaking scene in detail:

> At the festival Pilate used to release for the people a prisoner whom they requested. There was one named Barabbas, who was in prison with rebels who had committed murder during the rebellion. The crowd came up and began to ask Pilate to do for them as was his custom. Pilate answered them, "Do you want me to release the king of the Jews for you?" For he knew it was because of envy that the chief priests had handed him over. But the chief priests stirred up the crowd so that he would release Barabbas to them instead. Pilate asked them again, "Then what do you want me to do with the one you call the king of the Jews?" Again they shouted, "Crucify him!" Pilate said to them, "Why? What has he done wrong?" But they shouted all the more, "Crucify him!" (Mark 15:6–14)

Throughout each Gospel account, we see Pilate coming to terms with the undeniable truth of Jesus's innocence. Pilate even understands the motivation behind Jesus's persecution, its roots in envy and power. In the hours leading up to this moment, Pilate has used reason to sort out truth from perception. He has stood amazed at Jesus's response to what Pilate knows is an unjust, unwarranted arrest. So, why didn't he just release him?

The story of Pilate on Good Friday is a story of what happens when sin has taken root. Living your life in such a way that you honor yourself above all others can allow sin to go unchecked. For Pilate, the opportunity to free an innocent man, to act in a manner in line with truth and reason, arose on Good Friday. And Pilate knew it. When the crowds yelled out for Barabbas to be freed, he responded with confusion, "Why?" The demands of the crowd did not align with the undeniable truth before him. The willing departure from reason seems to have shaken Pilate, yet standing for truth would cost more than he was willing to pay.

Throughout his political career, Pilate had led with extreme aggression. He was brutal and ruthless, seeking power, control, and self-gain above all else—so much so that he found himself in trouble with Emperor Tiberius. The emperor had received one too many complaints about Pilate, and now his future was a bit uncertain. He was laden with sin, and the very power his sin had created was on the brink of falling away. Pilate knew he was in a precarious position, and so did the Pharisees. Because of this, the Pharisees were able to manipulate Pilate into a complacent bystander. Pilate's career could not weather one more misstep. The religious leadership had set up Jesus as a criminal against Rome with the charges they pursued. This meant that to grant amnesty to Jesus would be turning a blind eye to the crime against Rome, against the emperor. Yet Pilate's conscience could not be settled as he turned his back on what was happening to Jesus.

Charles Spurgeon brilliantly describes Pilate's problem like this:

> Pilate's transgressions were now howling around him like a pack of wolves; he could not face them, and he did not have the grace to flee to the one great refuge; but his fears drove him to flee before them, and there was no way apparently open for him except what led him into even deeper abominations. He knew that Jesus was without a single fault, and yet since the Jews clamoured for his death he felt that he must yield to their demands, or else they would raise another accusation against

> him, namely, that he was not loyal to the sovereignty of Caesar, for he had allowed one to escape who had called himself a king. If he had behaved justly he would not have been afraid of the chief priests and Scribes. Innocence is brave; but guilt is cowardly. Pilate's old sins found him out and made him weak in the presence of the ignoble crew, whom otherwise he would have driven from the judgment seat. He had enough power to have silenced them, but he did not have sufficient decision of character to end the contention.[1]

It was the presence of the guilt and shame of his previous sins that placed Pilate in this precarious position. There seemed to be no way out of this situation, except turning his back on truth.

In his kindness, God showed Pilate that he had landed on the truth and that it would be the best to trust in faith and move forward. God affirmed that Pilate's sense of reason had indeed pointed him to the truth. As he sat on the judgment seat, facing the reality before him, there was a moment of intercession. And, as is the story so often in the Bible, God called upon a woman to step out boldly.

While Pilot was sitting on the judge's bench, his wife, quite unexpectedly, sent word to him: "Have nothing to do with that righteous man, for today I've suffered terribly in a dream because of him" (Matt. 27:19).

Claudia Procula, Pilate's wife, was the granddaughter of Emperor Augustus and thus a Roman princess. She represented great political power to her husband, their marriage having been arranged to his favor. We know Pilate was in Jerusalem on special assignment to watch over the Passover festival. For a wife to accompany a governor to such an assignment was highly unusual

[1] A sermon delivered on Sunday Morning, February 26, 1882, by C. H. Spurgeon, at the Metropolitan Tabernacle, Newington, UK.

and more than likely required a special provision by Tiberius. The permission was likely granted because of how respected she was by both her husband and Tiberius. While her very presence in Jerusalem was an anomaly, even more so was the respect and affection she and her husband seemingly had for each other.

At this time in history in particular, a woman interrupting any formal proceeding was shocking. This required a boldness and urgency that came from God himself. There has been much speculation about the details of Claudia's dream. Scripture doesn't provide us with any specifics about what in the dream was so disturbing. Whatever the content, it was enough to stir her to send a warning and to implore her husband.

It is important to note how she describes Jesus: "righteous." She is not only asking for him to be left alone but also confirming his innocence. Claudia is the only one that declared his innocence *and* attempted to intervene. She stepped out bravely. And all because of the dream she had.

That dream was a demonstration of the intercession that comes from God. From time to time, we may be the recipient of those messages of warning. When facing a path that seems to lead in only one direction, when it seems that the only way out of our mess is to keep on sinning, God can remind us there is another way. This was the gift given to Pilate. A reminder that reason points to the truth.

And yet Pilate couldn't, didn't follow through on the truth he had reasoned and then had affirmed. Perhaps he perceived the cost of turning away from his sin and pointing to the truth to be too costly. Perhaps he perceived himself to be stuck with no way out. It is tragic to consider that he believed there was no way, when all along God was not only making a way but sending glaring warning signs to him.

The understanding that reason will point to faith is a shocking thing for a critical thinker to experience. A person who is a particularly astute critical thinker can easily convince themselves that the only way to faith is by letting go of reason—this is so far from the truth. Realizing that reason, truth, and faith all point to the same place is a revelation. And when a critical thinker comes face-to-face with the undeniable truth of who God is, it can easily upend them.

In a recent interview with Jonathan Pageau, the acclaimed and somewhat notorious Canadian clinical psychologist Jordan Peterson found himself upended in such a way. As Peterson was discussing the ramifications of the intersection of the spiritual world, he was suddenly overcome. Known for his cutting rationale and deductions, this great thinker had just reasoned his way into a face-to-face confrontation with the truth. He was breathless. As he began to speak after a moment of silence, tears began to stream as he verbalized the internal struggle that occurs when reason points somewhere unexpected—to faith:

> I am amazed at my own belief, and I don't understand it. . . . I believe it is undeniable. The narrative and objective world touch. The ultimate example of that in principle is supposed to be Christ. That seems to me oddly plausible. I don't know what to make of it. Partly because it's too terrifying a reality to fully believe. I don't even know what would happen to you if you fully believed it.[2]

Peterson gave words to the struggle Pilate found himself in. The reality is too terrifying. Pilate knew the truth. He saw the envy of the Pharisees, the manipulation of the crowd, and the innocence of Jesus. His personal judgment, his reason, brought him to that

[2] "The Perfect Mode of Being | Jonathan Pageau - Jordan B. Peterson Podcast S4 E8," YouTube, March 1, 2021, https://www.youtube.com/watch?v=2rAqVmZwqZM&t=1466s.

realization. Yet he turned his back on it. Perhaps it was because he was not ready to face the terrifying reality of his own sin and the God who had come to die for him.

We are not called to turn our backs on reason to experience the fullness of faith. It is okay to be like Pilate and ask questions like, "Does this align with the truth?" The beauty of the Christian faith is that it does not require an abandoning of reason. It requires sacrifice, yes, but among the sacrifices is never the suspension of our own critical thought.

Given the choice between the true Son of God and the other Bar Abba, Pilate ultimately made the easier and more tragic choice. Barabbas was free and Christ was headed to the cross. The imitation is always the easier choice. The imitation allows us to hold on to our sin. Yet truth and reason don't point to the imitation; they point to the true Son of God. We know that the freedom Barabbas found that day was not actual freedom, just as we know that Christ did experience freedom on Good Friday. And in his doing so, he bought it for us all.

But at this moment on Good Friday, the moment of Pilate's ultimate decision, we don't see the joy of freedom, truth, reason, and faith coming together. Pilate is another tragic figure of this heavy day, much like Judas. They allowed more space for their past sin, and sin's preferred companions of shame and deceit, than they made room for truth, reason, and hope. May we step out in faith with confidence that reason and truth lead us to the same place, to freedom.

Via Dolorosa Way of Grief

As we follow Jesus from Gethsemane to Golgotha and then to the tomb, take a few moments to sit quietly with him. Similar to the Way of the Cross or Stations of the Cross, we will pause to reflect on the moments and meaning of Good Friday. There is grief in death. But there is also grief in our sin and in our misalignment with God. Before we continue on, we must pause and grieve.

REFLECT

- Have you thought reason has a place in a life of faith, or have you held reason and faith in two separate worlds?
- Have you experienced moments of God using another person to help you change course? Did you welcome or resist it?
- As you reflect, ask God to reveal his presence and will. What does he show you?

CONFESS

- Are you willing to change your mind even when it may cause you peril?
- Do you believe truth and reason point to a life of faith?

- Where is there misalignment in your desires, actions, and thoughts?

- Where are you not valuing what Jesus valued?

RECONSIDER

- Letting go of our will and seeking God's will is the way to freedom, beauty, and life.
- The redemptive work begins with letting go of control.
- Take time to pray and affirm this.

PART THREE

Reimagining

As Jesus, flogged and beaten, begins the walk to Golgotha, the place of his crucifixion—as he makes his way there, is crucified, and draws his last breath—we see death to self brought to life in new and surprising ways. Lay aside any pretense you have for what this means and instead see these next few hours in a new way. A life surrendered may require a reimagining of what it looks like to follow Christ.

CHAPTER SEVEN

WHO AM I?

Death of Entitlement

Simon Carries the Cross

Matthew 27:32 | Mark 15:21 | Luke 23:26

Of all the things we wrangle into our control, it is somewhat disheartening and humbling to realize that even the way we approach service falls prey to the fist-clenching nature of wielding control in our own lives. Often, we control what we serve, how we serve, and even who we serve. The root of this is a sense of assuredness that not only do we know best, but we even know who we can best bless.

We forge ahead with our planned service, written in our calendar, set up in advance, entirely convinced we are doing the good work God has called us to. While we may hold awareness of how we can step into others' lives in service, oftentimes we miss the fact that our service is meant to shape us much more than it is ever meant to shape those we serve.

It is in the *unplanned* moments of service that God shows up in our lives, causes us to turn around, and asks of us, "Are you willing to change directions and allow me to shape you?" This is what we see as we look at Simon of Cyrene:

> As they were going out, they met a man from Cyrene, named Simon, and they forced him to carry the cross. (Matt. 27:32 NIV)

> A certain man from Cyrene, Simon, the father of Alexander and Rufus, was passing by on his way in from the country, and they forced him to carry the cross. (Mark 15:21 NIV)

> As the soldiers led him away, they seized Simon from Cyrene, who was on his way in from the country, and put the cross on him and made him carry it behind Jesus. (Luke 23:26 NIV)

As Jesus makes his way outside the city to the place of his death, he starts to falter under the weight of the cross. He stumbles and falls. The weight is too much for his broken body. This presents a problem for the Roman soldiers, who need the cross to arrive at the site to complete the crucifixion. It was inconceivable that a Roman soldier would have lifted it, not because of the weight of the crossbar (approximately 75–125 pounds) but because to carry a cross is to carry the mark of humiliation.

Roman soldiers, by law, had the right to force civilians into labor, a practice that often manifested itself in citizens being forced to carry the soldiers' gear.[1] However, on this day, this practice manifested itself in the soldiers picking someone to carry Jesus's cross. And thus we meet Simon.

---

[1]Craig S. Keener, *The IVP Bible Background Commentary: New Testament* (Downers Grove, IL: InterVarsity Press, 2014), 59.

Simon was presumably in the area for the Passover festival, having come from Cyrene on the northern coast of Africa. This morning, he was headed back into the city. This is an important detail. Simon was heading *into* the city as Jesus and the soldiers were headed *out* of the city into the countryside of Golgotha. However, the soldiers stopped Simon and forced him to carry Jesus's cross. When Simon picked up that crossbar, he turned around 180 degrees and headed in the opposite direction he had been moving.

This is the kind of service that changes us—unexpected, inconvenient, and unplanned—often requiring of us, as it did of Simon, to make an about-face and to completely change directions.

Imagine walking down the dusty road to Jerusalem, excited to celebrate the coming festival, and walking right into a scene like Simon saw? He was forced, compelled, to stop what he was doing and step into that situation. How do you handle that type of interruption?

For most of us, our first reaction is one rooted in entitlement.

"This is not what I was planning."

"I don't have the time."

"This is not my problem."

In other words, "I do not deserve to be bogged down in this; I am owed something easier, more rewarding, less invasive."

Or even, "Why me?!"

We have all been there.

In that early spring of 2007, when I received the frantic phone call from my sister alerting me that our mom was on the way to the hospital, the day we learned of her diagnosis from the callous ER doctor, I had just pulled into my driveway. That phone call led to a long thirteen months of saying goodbye to our mom, who actually had an aggressive form of brain cancer. The day I received the phone call, I got in my car and drove to my mom's house, where my brother, sister, and dad were. Unbeknownst to me at the time, I had just moved from our little log cabin in the Berkshires of Massachusetts to my new role as family caretaker in Upstate New York.

Deciding to show up to care for my mom, and by extension my family, my dad and brother in particular, was the easiest thing I have ever done. There was no decision, no hesitation. It was grueling and heavy and all the things caregiving for someone is, but it was never a hard decision. After all, it was my mom. She held all things together for us, and serving someone who has done everything for you is not particularly noble but is instead a mere attempt at reciprocity. As I said, it never felt like a sacrifice or even a stretch.

When Mom passed away, in May 2008, my teenage brother was on the verge of graduating from high school and heading to college, while my dad was carrying on with his own brain injury and several other ailments leaving him incapable of living on his own. My husband, Josh, had moved into the family home shortly after I did the previous year to help with the family. And we had just welcomed our son into the mix. So there we were—newborn, college-aged sibling, and Dad, all on our shoulders.

And that is exactly when the resentment tried to creep in.

While moving in to care for my mom was a no-brainer, staying to take care of things after she passed was a different situation. Caring for someone with a terminal illness was very different from caring for someone indefinitely. I was shocked that God had me in this position where, at thirty, I had already buried my biological father[2] and my mother, and was left with the only parent who was not even capable of parenting due to a brain injury. I had already

[2]Not to overcomplicate things, but my "Father" is my birth father and my "Dad" (Osh) is technically my stepdad. My biological father spent minimal time with me throughout my life, but my dad (Osh) was ever-present from two years old on.

stepped in to serve. Surely I had been formed enough that I could now move on to a new season. Right?

Wrong.

I don't remember the particulars of our decision-making process in those months after Mom passed. I was aware that I wanted my brother to be able to come home to his own home during college break. I was aware that life in a facility would be the worst thing for Osh. But what about me? What about what I was owed? That's when Josh stepped in to proclaim a truth that changed everything.

We were standing in the hallway between my brother and Osh's bedrooms, and Josh said to me, "I never would have guessed this a few years ago, but your calling is to take care of this family. It is where God has placed you, and it's not done yet." I am not sure how to explain the peace I felt in that moment. Josh's observations, which could have been suffocating or stifling, condemning even, were instead totally and completely life-giving.

From that moment, I stopped looking at my service as time served and instead began asking God, "What do you want to change in me through this?" It was in that shedding of entitlement, or being stuck on what I deserved, that God began to shape me. Yes, *began*. My time spent caring for my mom was beautiful. I would not change those thirteen months for the world. But that was self-imposed service. God was there, without question. But the shaping began when I was left to serve where I would never have chosen to be.

The amazing thing is that Jesus himself spoke about bitterness in this scenario: "And if anyone forces you to go one mile, go with him two. Give to the one who asks you, and don't turn away from the one who wants to borrow from you" (Matt. 5:41–42). Here, "one mile" is again referring to the Roman soldier's authority over civilians. It was commonplace for a Roman soldier to force a man to carry his pack for up to a mile. Jesus's answer to the call of "Why me?!" was to not serve as mandated but, instead, serve double. The best way to take off the robes of entitlement is to serve and serve wholeheartedly.

Jesus was serious about service. Why, then, do we believe he doesn't want to use service to shape us? It won't happen if we cut him off. We must allow ourselves to be disrupted by his call on our lives to serve.

Of course, this is not to say that planned service is a bad thing. It is a way the church moves and enacts change. Planned service is a way to help others and use our gifts. The problem arises when planned service is the only service we participate in. If we hold too tightly to our idea of what service is, when it works in our lives, and who we are called to serve, then we will likely miss the opportunity to be shaped by the "unplanned" service that has been ordained just for us and our good. Beyond this, we just might deny ourselves the life-changing honor of serving Christ himself.

Here is what I know to be true: living a life open to serving others in unplanned ways *will* change you—and change you in impactful ways. My shift from being self-centered to being compassionate can be credited to caring for my dad for over ten years. It has been the way I have been shaped by Jesus the most. It also provided an opening within my soul to consider a softer, gentler way to be. From that has come so much additional spiritual growth. The fertile ground for all those seeds was tilled in my willingness to be changed by the service I never expected.

Although Simon was compelled by the Romans, he could have easily allowed resentment and entitlement to come over him. Had that been the case, he likely would have walked away from his hour of service unchanged. There is evidence to suggest this is not the case. Some speculate Simon may, in fact, have been involved in planting a church at Antioch or involved in the movement in

Cyrene.[3] In particular, the book of Acts makes this amazing statement: "But there were some of them, men from Cyprus and Cyrene, who came to Antioch and began speaking to the Greeks also, proclaiming the good news about the Lord Jesus" (Acts 11:20). Was Simon involved in this? We don't know for sure. But what we do know is that the church in Cyprus was on fire and that believers (possibly Simon) were bold enough to preach to the Greeks! This led to the creation of the Antioch church, which is the church responsible for sending the Apostle Paul out as a missionary.[4]

I believe that all these great happenings in the early church are linked to Simon. Imagine the testimony he shared when he came back to Cyrene after that Passover weekend? Even more so, imagine what Simon's experience changed in him. The service ordained for us is designed to shift and shape us.

I can personally attest to this. Serving, for me, has shifted things within my own heart—it grew patience where it was in short supply, increased my dependency on God, and cultivated a death to myself and my entitlement that I pray will stay with me forever.

When we look once more at the verse in Mark (15:21), we see another blessing that occurs when we welcome unplanned service. The people who watch us are changed. In a highly uncharacteristic manner, Mark mentions not just Simon by name but also his sons, Rufus and Alexander. Why would the author do that?

As a bit of background, the Gospel of Mark was written by John Mark, cousin to Barnabas and companion to both his cousin and the Apostle Paul. Some even believe that the upper room where the Last Supper was celebrated was, in fact, in John Mark's mother's home. John Mark primarily wrote for the Roman Gentiles and was

---

[3] "Simon of Cyrene," The Bible Study, accessed August 11, 2021, https://thebiblestudy.co.uk/study/simon-of-cyrene/.

[4] Craig S. Keener, *The IVP Bible Background Commentary: New Testament* (Downers Grove, IL: InterVarsity Press, 2014), 354.

quite involved in the church of Rome. It is important to remember these accounts are deeply personal. The writer is connected and known to both the subjects and the intended readers.

Also involved in the Roman church was Simon's grown son, Rufus. By the time this Gospel was recorded, the church in Rome was growing. Rufus was well-known and revered—so much so that in his letter to the Romans, Paul says, "Greet Rufus, chosen in the Lord; also his mother—and mine" (Rom. 16:13).

The mention of Rufus and his brother in the account of Simon carrying Jesus's cross validates the events. It is John Mark's way of saying, "You know Rufus. Ask him about what happened to his dad! It's amazing!" Even further, the life Rufus was leading was one of great servitude to the church. The impact of the turning around of Simon made its way not just back to Cyrene, then Antioch, and the whole world through Paul, but also through Simon's sons and their own work in servitude to the gospel of Jesus Christ.

As someone who raised children in the midst of unplanned service, I take great comfort in this. I have often wondered what impact our serving will have on our kids. We have said no to a lot of things because of the needs of those who were in our care. We have had to pass on many of the typical kid activities because of the constraints of our larger family structure. Our children have watched their mom and dad rotate shifts at hospitals and nursing homes as we would come and go at crazy hours. They know what it is like to negotiate seizures and strokes and dementia and great loss. But there is also this: Our kids know how to delight in a nursing home. They know how to show up to help family. And they know that joy can still exist at the cemetery. They know what it looks like to strip off the sense of what is owed to them and instead be open to the needs around them.

I know our children are already equipped to serve in big ways. I see them do it often, alongside us, with each other, with strangers.

They are world changers. Just today, we helped a stranger in the park. A woman was protesting and ranting and generally losing her cool. She walked by us, first mumbling and then shouting in outrage. Just then, a burst of wind scattered her poster boards across the park as if they were the seeds of a dandelion blown about. Many had been watching her, as she had been ranting just a moment prior to the gust of wind. But, as the woman was frantically gathering what had been lost from her grip, there was no one who would make eye contact with her. I began to work alongside her gathering her signs, and my kids immediately jumped up and followed suit. I hadn't said a word to them. Not only that, but following their example, their friends began to join in as well.

I handed the posterboards back to the woman, who I learned was named Penny, and asked how her day was. We had a five-minute conversation that rambled from one conspiracy theory to another in stream-of-consciousness fashion, as she shared with me all her concerns. It was a calm and gentle conversation. As I wished her well and turned back to my kids, she too turned to go about her afternoon . . . and began ranting at top volume once again. It was jarring. One of the friends with us looked a bit downtrodden as he realized our moment of being a good Samaritan was rewarded with foul language and aggressive shouts. Before I could even say anything, my eight-year-old son, Finley, said, "Don't worry. We help people just because it's good to help them, not because they act perfect. It's good to help for no reason at all."

This is what it sounds like to live welcoming the unplanned moments of service. If welcoming that in our own lives can not only change our lives but also the lives of those around us, what are we waiting for?! We may never know the full effects of this until we reach heaven. But we for sure can see how it will allow us to see the world as a place of opportunity. Each day presents a new opportunity for us to be turned around by Jesus himself as we are called to step into service and let go of the sense that we are too entitled to serve another. May we welcome the transformative nature of unplanned service.

Via Dolorosa Way of Grief

As we follow Jesus from Gethsemane to Golgotha and then to the tomb, take a few moments to sit quietly with him. Similar to the Way of the Cross or Stations of the Cross, we will pause to reflect on the moments and meaning of Good Friday. There is grief in death. But there is also grief in our sin and in our misalignment with God. Before we continue on, we must pause and grieve.

REFLECT

- Do you welcome unplanned service?

- As you reflect, ask God to reveal his presence and will. What does he show you?

CONFESS

- Have you held yourself to scheduled service?
- How do you handle interruptions?
- Where is there misalignment in your desires, actions, and thoughts?
- Where are you not valuing what Jesus valued?

RECONSIDER

- Letting go of our will and seeking God's will is the way to freedom, beauty, and life.
- The redemptive work begins with letting go of control.
- Take time to pray and affirm this.

CHAPTER EIGHT

CARE FOR OTHERS

Death of Distress

Jesus Speaks to the Daughters of Jerusalem

Luke 23:28–31

After Simon picked up the crossbeam and walked with Jesus, maybe even moments after, Jesus speaks to the women walking along with them to the place of his crucifixion. Jesus, who a moment ago was so battered he could not carry the crossbeam, is now offering words of sympathy to the onlookers. Scripture tells us these women were mourning and lamenting what was happening to Jesus. I wonder what Simon thought as he heard Christ offer words of comfort. It is quite something to consider that one of the gifts of his saying yes to that unplanned service was being a witness to what Christ shared in these moments:

> But turning to them, Jesus said, "Daughters of Jerusalem, do not weep for me, but weep for yourselves and your children. Look, the days are coming when they will say,

> 'Blessed are the women without children, the wombs that never bore, and the breasts that never nursed!' Then they will begin to say to the mountains, 'Fall on us!' and to the hills, 'Cover us!' For if they do these things when the wood is green, what will happen when it is dry?" (Luke 23:28–31)

These words are often held, rightly so, as prophecy for the coming fall of Jerusalem. *The days are coming*, he warns, *when it will be violent and dangerous to be here*. And, of course, he was right. Jerusalem fell in AD 70 in a brutal siege.

Yet I wonder if there is another lesson for us here. We also see Jesus's response to his own physical pain—to think of and offer comfort to someone else. What Jesus shows us is a beautiful prescription to our own distress: care for others.

In a world that is so focused on self, this is a revolutionary idea. The answer to relieving our own suffering is to have compassion for someone else. How different would our world be if we spent our energy not on our own troubles but on empathizing with others? What would shift in our spirits if we, instead of focusing on our own distress, offered comfort to another?

Rather than an inward focus, we see an outward focus in Jesus's words to the women. "Do not weep for me," Jesus tells them. In other words, he is saying, "I'm not worried about me, I am worried about you." His physical state is not changed; he is still experiencing great pain. And yet there appears to be a lack of distress.

I have experienced both the relief that comes from such focus and the sting that comes from a self-centered approach to distress. In the days immediately following my mom's initial diagnosis, her brothers, my uncles, began to arrive. My uncles were not known for their gentleness or compassion, and in those first few tense days as we awaited surgery, that became very apparent. I was cornered by one of them in a hospital hallway as he began to tell me how distraught he was over my mom's diagnosis. I attempted to meet him with compassion but struggled to do so. He was going on and on about how tragic this situation was *for him*. And then, leaving no opportunity for misinterpretation, he said, "I know it's your mom, but it's *my sister*!" I was shocked. And hurt. I stood there thinking, *Where is the compassion? For her children; for her husband with an existing brain injury?*

The selfishness, the self-focus my uncle displayed in that moment, shook me. I was able to see from this occasion and many subsequent interactions with him how distress actually spreads when that kind of focus is present. And I was determined not to replicate it. My response was to focus on my then teenage brother. I was thirty, too young to say goodbye to my mom, but my brother was only seventeen. When I saw what he was facing, my distress lessened. It was the opposite response to my interaction with my uncle.

Focusing on those who need our care and compassion, through the goodness of God, actually lessens our own suffering.

I still faced the illness of my mom, the struggles that brought to me personally, and the heartache. But I can also testify that in my focus on what those around me needed, my own ache was tended to. It is a beautiful reality of surrendering our distress rather than focusing solely on ourselves.

I realize now that was the beginning of a shift in my focus that has changed everything for me. When facing a crisis, focusing on the most vulnerable will lessen our troubles. This principle has allowed my husband and me to walk through innumerable struggles with perspective that is aligned with Jesus. Our distress is minimized through the genuine care and concern for others.

This is not the role of a martyr but rather a welcoming of an unlikely remedy of our own distress. Care and concern for the most vulnerable will grant a greater peace to all involved. If we can let go of our own distress, we will find there is a deep well of comfort available, enough to minister to our hearts as well as the ones we care for.

Jesus affirms within his words to the women that day that we will have tribulation, a confirmation of trouble to come. But I also see a way to move through the unavoidable trials of life with less distress and more awareness of his care. The answer is found in those first words of verse twenty-eight: "But turning to them." Turn to those in need. Turn to those in lament and mourning. Moments before, the story was about the help Jesus needed to carry the cross; but then it became a new story as Jesus began ministering care and concern. May this be our story as well.

Via Dolorosa Way of Grief

As we follow Jesus from Gethsemane to Golgotha and then to the tomb, take a few moments to sit quietly with him. Similar to the Way of the Cross or Stations of the Cross, we will pause to reflect on the moments and meaning of Good Friday. There is grief in death. But there is also grief in our sin and in our misalignment with God. Before we continue on, we must pause and grieve.

REFLECT

- What do you notice about Jesus's response to the women?

- As you reflect, ask God to reveal his presence and will. What does he show you?

CONFESS

- Do you focus on your own distress?
- Are there those for whom you could be demonstrating care?
- Where is there misalignment in your desires, actions, and thoughts?
- Where are you not valuing what Jesus valued?

RECONSIDER

- Letting go of our will and seeking God's will is the way to freedom, beauty, and life.
- The redemptive work begins with letting go of control.
- Take time to pray and affirm this.

CHAPTER NINE

ADVOCATING FORGIVENESS

Death of Revenge

Jesus Forgives

Luke 23:33–43

We all know that forgiving others is important. We know that Jesus himself called for it and perfectly modeled it. So why is it so difficult?

We arrive at Golgotha, known also as The Skull and Calvary. Each name comes from the Greek word *kranion*. It is here that Jesus is crucified. I think as Matthew, Mark, Luke, and John recorded their accounts, they were keenly aware that the act of crucifixion was the least amazing thing that happened that day—so it is mentioned plainly, simply, and with brevity. But, then, we see Jesus use his time on the cross to teach some amazing lessons in a new way.

> When they arrived at the place called The Skull, they crucified him there, along with the criminals, one on the right and one on the left. Then Jesus said, "Father,

> forgive them, because they do not know what they are doing." And they divided his clothes and cast lots. (Luke 23:33–34)

Jesus's first act as a crucified man was to demonstrate an utter lack of vengefulness. Instead, he advocates for forgiveness.

There are many interpretations of who Jesus is directly referencing in Luke 23:34. Perhaps it is the soldiers standing guard, perhaps the religious leaders looking on, perhaps the criminals hanging next to him, or perhaps the statement is obtuse with intention. It could be the soldier who nailed him to the cross, it could be the Pharisees or Pilate, or it could be you and me.

The most striking thing about this scene is that Jesus advocated for forgiveness when there was no apparent repentance. This is where our understanding of control, expectations, and once again entitlement knock headfirst into what living surrendered in Christ looks like.

Forgiveness, when there is repentance, costs us little and offers no opportunity to shape us. It's also my preferred means of forgiving, as it comes easy and everything gets tied up in a neat bow. You harmed me, you are sorry, I forgive. Then we all can move on in peace and harmony. But this is not what we see on the cross.

We see Jesus relinquishing any notion of revenge and instead praying for forgiveness on behalf of those who demonstrate no remorse. How can we possibly be open enough to do that in our own lives?

The answer can be found, I believe, in the next interaction between Jesus and the two criminals.

> Then one of the criminals hanging there began to yell insults at him: "Aren't you the Messiah? Save yourself and us!" But the other answered, rebuking him: "Don't you even fear God, since you are undergoing the same

> punishment? We are punished justly, because we're getting back what we deserve for the things we did, but this man has done nothing wrong." Then he said, "Jesus, remember me when you come into your kingdom." And he said to him, "Truly I tell you, today you will be with me in paradise." (Luke 23:39–43)

The second criminal, recognizing who Jesus is, simply says, "Remember me." He makes no confession, he demonstrates no regret; he simply asks Jesus to remember him. Amazingly, Jesus responds with an assurance indicative of the ultimate forgiveness, confirming that the man will be in paradise together with him. This is the freedom of Christ's forgiveness—paradise, together.

This criminal knows what is owed him. There is no pretense of being falsely accused or unjustly crucified. He does not argue against his punishment. Instead, he asks to be remembered. I believe this is what is asked of us as we are called to forgive here on the earth. We forgive because first we remember. We remember that all are sinners—ourselves included. We remember that we are all owed nothing except punishment. We also remember what we have been forgiven for.

This is widely counterintuitive. In our flesh, we remember. We remember wrongs. We remember hurtful words, sinful actions. We remember how such things affected us, or those we love. This recordkeeping of wrongs does nothing but hold us captive in a pit of entitlement and superiority.

We find joy and delight, and most of all fellowship, with Jesus when we remember that all are children of God—beloved and longed for. When given the choice between joy and delight or entitlement and bitterness, let's choose wisely.

I grew up in a home that did not place special items in a place of great austerity. There was no such thing as "the good furniture" reserved for the adults or special company. I, for the most part, adopted the same mentality—a house is meant to be lived in.

Except, I did have a handblown glass lamp that I cherished. The lamp came from an artisan that I admired for a long time and was truly delighted to have such a piece of art in my home. I thought my adoration for this lamp was in check, admiring the beauty of the craftsmanship without making an idol. I had moved the lamp from our bedroom, where it was seldom used but certainly kept safe, to our sitting room, a place with very high traffic. As I placed the lamp down, my husband offered a word of caution. I scoffed and reminded him that things are meant to be enjoyed. Here, in its new location, I would be able to appreciate the lamp more, and after all, "It's just a thing."

It sat in that room for almost a year . . . until our kids broke it.

First I heard the crash. Then I heard the gasps. Then one brave child came up to my office to share the news. The lamp had fallen, but, although slightly out of her sight, she thought it was okay. I attempted, and failed, to not look horrified, took a few breaths, and then said I would be right down. The kids had scattered, awaiting my inspection. It was, in fact, broken and completely so.

After a few more deep breaths, I knew that forgiveness was required. By all accounts, this was an accident that did not even require consequences. So I removed the evidence of the lamp that was and called the kids back into the room. I let them know that there would be no consequences, and that while we could not replace this lamp, I could find something affordable at Target to light up their reading table.

They agreed and moved on with their day as if nothing of consequence had just happened. They received my grand gesture of mercy and forgiveness as if it hadn't just cost me a tremendous sacrifice. I was dumbfounded! For the next few hours, they went about their day with joy and delight, but I was seething.

My self-righteous posture of offering such a gift as forgiveness was confronted with my children's indifference to that very thing. I wrestled with the Lord quite a bit that afternoon. My cries went from, "How can my children be so ungrateful?" to "How could I place so much value in a lamp?!" I was humbled and disheartened to see what a grip it had on me.

And that is when I realized the true purpose of forgiveness. It has nothing to do with the other person. The act of truly forgiving, in Christ, just as he did, is all about our own freedom. That's the thing about forgiveness—*aphiēmi* in Greek. The word *aphiēmi* is used to convey not only the concept of forgiveness but also letting go, departing, fleeing.

Forgiveness is by its very nature an act of letting go of what has its grip on you. It is saying, to bitterness, resentment, and revenge, "Flee from me." The freedom you can experience in forgiving another is available to you at all times. This is why the notion that we are called to forgive even in the absence of repentance is so critical. Your freedom has nothing to do with another's actions but has everything to do with your willingness to follow Jesus.

It is no mistake that this is the first thing Jesus does after being nailed to the cross. He shows us all that we do not need to be bound up in bitterness. Imagine the freedom we can possess by welcoming the opportunity to let go, to *aphiēmi*.

As he was raised on the cross, Jesus began to pray, "Father, forgive them." May we live our lives in the same way so that we can pray with assurance as Jesus taught in the Lord's Prayer, "Forgive us our debts, as we also have forgiven our debtors" (Matt. 6:12). That is a bold prayer Jesus asserted for his disciples to learn. Imagine asking to be forgiven to the measure we offer forgiveness. The stinging of that verse can easily be replaced with delight and freedom if we would only follow him, advocate for forgiveness, and cause revenge to flee.

Via Dolorosa Way of Grief

As we follow Jesus from Gethsemane to Golgotha and then to the tomb, take a few moments to sit quietly with him. Similar to the Way of the Cross or Stations of the Cross, we will pause to reflect on the moments and meaning of Good Friday. There is grief in death. But there is also grief in our sin and in our misalignment with God. Before we continue on, we must pause and grieve.

REFLECT

- What do you notice about the forgiveness Jesus demonstrates?

- Does your forgiveness have caveats?

- As you reflect, ask God to reveal his presence and will. What does he show you?

CONFESS

- Have you held on to resentment?

- Are there those who you need to forgive?

- Where is there misalignment in your desires, actions, and thoughts?

- Where are you not valuing what Jesus valued?

RECONSIDER

- Letting go of our will and seeking God's will is the way to freedom, beauty, and life.
- The redemptive work begins with letting go of control.
- Take time to pray and affirm this.

CHAPTER TEN

IT'S JUST A NAME

Death of Earthly Titles

Titulus Placed on Cross

Matthew 27:27–31, 37 | Mark 15:16–20, 26 | Luke 23:35–38 | John 19:19–22

Like it or not, our world is full of labels. We use labels to categorize people, for better or for worse. We welcome some labels on ourselves while we do our best to keep our distance from others. Some titles we wear with honor, and others we shirk from. Similarly, we elevate some people based on their titles while condemning others. Despite the weight we assign to them, the labels that we all walk around with, invisibly floating above our heads, carries no weight when they are grounded in earthly understanding.

The label given to Jesus as he was crucified is unique in that it was assigned as a means of mockery yet holds the ultimate truth. The sign above his head begs us to ask the question of which labels matter and why.

> Pilate also had a sign made and put on the cross. It said: Jesus of Nazareth, the King of the Jews. Many

> of the Jews read this sign, because the place where Jesus was crucified was near the city, and it was written in Aramaic, Latin, and Greek. So the chief priests of the Jews said to Pilate, "Don't write, 'The king of the Jews,' but that he said, 'I am the king of the Jews.'" Pilate replied, "What I have written, I have written." (John 19:19–22)

The word "title" as used here derives from the Latin word *titulus*. *Titulus* is the name for the wooden sign mentioned here in John's Gospel but also for the criminal charge itself. Often, this plaque bearing the charge against the one being crucified would be carried through the street as a means of intimidation or warning. The *titulus* was a public decree of guilt and punishment—an awful kind of "I am" statement designed to mortify the criminal and be a word of warning to any observing the procession to crucifixion. Woe to anyone who schemed to take part in the same type of crime.

Here we see this also being a moment of Pilate exerting his power over the Jewish Pharisees. Pilate rightly deemed Jesus's crime to be that he was Jesus of Nazareth, King of the Jews. The priests responded that the crime, as they saw it (or had convinced themselves of), was not that Jesus *was* the King of the Jews, but that he had *claimed* to be. Pilate won't back down, and so this *titulus*, this title, gets nailed to the cross above Jesus for all to see.

Did Pilate know he was for certain the King, the Messiah? Perhaps so. It seems at the least he knew the motives of the religious leaders. Pilate was uneasy about this whole thing. Remember his interactions with Jesus, the Pharisees, and even his own wife? The title, as Pilate assigned it, seemed to point out not so much the charge against Jesus as the crime of the Pharisees.

This title hanging over Jesus holds many meanings yet is simultaneously meaningless. And this is exactly how we ought to consider titles today. They can hold much meaning yet ultimately no meaning. It all depends if it is a title based on earthly striving or if the title instead is from God. The title of King from the earthly perspective of the Roman law and the religious leaders is a title that causes condemnation and, even further, is not the role Jesus sought or possessed. Yet it is the title assigned him, by man. And the earthly title was actually convoluting the reality of who Jesus actually was and is, King of Heaven.

Our response to earthly titles is one worthy of inspection. Do we place too much significance on the titles of others? Do we place favor and merit where there is simply a man-made label? Even more important, how attached are we to our own labels? Do we draw lines around something based on what we claim to be when God may desire to instead move us beyond that boundary?

A few years ago, we were called to switch the course of our kids' schooling. We felt it was time to try homeschooling. The only problem was, I was not a "homeschooler." I loved school. I loved our kids' school. I loved being a part of the kids' school. I had never felt inclined to admonish those in my life who homeschooled, but I thought for sure, "That is for them but not for me." In other words, they bore the *titulus* "homeschool mom"; my *titulus* held another charge.

As I began to wrestle with this notion, I confided in a homeschooling friend, sharing my hesitation and with trepidation. How would it feel to put this title above my head? Was God really asking me to change my allegiance within the school system? In my head, I knew I was many things, but a homeschooler? It did not fit with how I perceived myself.

At the end of the conversation, my friend said the most astonishing thing to me: "You are already homeschooling." What?! She then went on to list several things I had been doing all along that did, in fact, point to the truth that I was already a homeschooler.

We took family field trips, we toured historic sites and art museums, we had read-alouds always going, and my kids were always doing picture narrations and a slew of other schooling activities, with me, at home. Homeschooling. It had been there all along.

How had I missed this?

I was worried about the stigma of homeschooling, yet my friend had lovingly seen where God was moving in my life. My desire to shrug off a label that I thought did not fit me had prevented me from realizing I was already living under the label—and not just living under but thriving in the most positive way. While I turned my nose up at the label, I had already taken on the role and loved it. I was reminded of both the meaning and the insignificance labels can hold.

This was a humbling realization. I had placed too much weight on these labels, to the point that I was blind to what was right in front of me. My pride had prevented me from stepping back with open hands, causing me to instead draw rigid boundaries around who I was and who I was not. In so doing, I had missed who God had made me to be and what role he was calling me to.

Pride can cause us to hold on to all sorts of things that fly in the face of what God has for us. Pride whispers in our ears that of course we know what is best for us—we know who we are and, if you are like me, who you aren't.

This plays out in my life often: I was never a runner, yet I have run in races; I was never a gardener, yet I have grown many things on our small plot of land; I was not a writer, yet now I write books. My prideful notion of who I was and even further what role I was qualified for almost blocked me in each of these examples from tremendous blessings, tremendous personal growth, and a reliance on God that has shaped me profoundly. All because I believed I was the sole arbiter of my titles.

I have found much joy in letting go of using the world's standards, labels, or titles to define me. There is so much pressure in the world to label yourself in any number of ways. There are entire classes on crafting the most effective social media bio. There are rankings (seen and unseen) based on your following, your cliques, what groups you belong to. Are you a crunchy-hippie-oily mama or are you a tiger mom? Do you belong to the right or the left, progressive or conservative? Are you one of us or one of *them*? This is how the world considers people. But the earthly labels we put on or accept hold no eternal value.

If we are to let go of the notion that we choose our titles and the honor they bear on our lives, we must begin by recognizing that what the world calls one thing, the kingdom of God calls another. Where the world calls for strength, the kingdom calls for humility; where the world calls for striving, the kingdom calls for serving.

If that is true, why do we pay any mind to earthly titles?

During the Sermon on the Mount, Jesus begins with a list of blessings called the Beatitudes. This is what it looks like to hold favor in the kingdom of God:

> Blessed are the poor in spirit,
> for the kingdom of heaven is theirs.
> Blessed are those who mourn,
> for they will be comforted.
> Blessed are the humble,
> for they will inherit the earth.
> Blessed are those who hunger and thirst
> for righteousness,
> for they will be filled.
> Blessed are the merciful,
> for they will be shown mercy.

> Blessed are the pure in heart,
> for they will see God.
> Blessed are the peacemakers,
> for they will be called sons of God.
> Blessed are those who are persecuted because
> of righteousness,
> for the kingdom of heaven is theirs. (Matt. 5:3–10)

This list of blessings does not make sense in the context of the world. How could it? Jesus is painting a picture of what it looks like to live in unity with him. The poor are rich, the mourners are comforted, and the hungry are fed. The world does not understand a leader who is a servant. The world does not understand a person who welcomes death as a means for life. We can hold earthly titles with an open hand, knowing they offer us no value compared to the title of being blessed in the kingdom. We are in the world, but we do not hold ourselves to the world's standards.

The beautiful thing about the *titulus* hanging above Jesus's head is this: though it was created to mock and scorn, it actually pointed to eternal truth. "Here is Jesus, King of the Jews, condemned criminal." But also, "Here is Jesus, King of the Jews, dying for our freedom, for mine and yours." Here is my King.

May we let go of earthly titles and instead seek out what God has for us, knowing the labels of the Kingdom of God are the only ones that matter.

Via Dolorosa Way of Grief

As we follow Jesus from Gethsemane to Golgotha and then to the tomb, take a few moments to sit quietly with him. Similar to the Way of the Cross or Stations of the Cross, we will pause to reflect on the moments and meaning of Good Friday. There is grief in death. But there is also grief in our sin and in our misalignment with God. Before we continue on, we must pause and grieve.

REFLECT

- What does the title of Jesus mean?

- Do you place too much value in labels?

- As you reflect, ask God to reveal his presence and will. What does he show you?

CONFESS

- Have you held yourself to a label?

- Do you rank yourself and others?

- Where is there misalignment in your desires, actions, and thoughts?

- Where are you not valuing what Jesus valued?

RECONSIDER

- Letting go of our will and seeking God's will is the way to freedom, beauty, and life.
- The redemptive work begins with letting go of control.
- Take time to pray and affirm this.

CHAPTER ELEVEN

REINVENTING RELATIONS

Death of the Ties That Bind

Jesus Trusts Mary to John

John 19:25–27

How can we be eternally focused yet deeply connected here on earth? The answer lies in how we relate to one another. Our eternal focus causes us to welcome service to one another while our willingness to be profoundly connected creates a rich family with fellow believers—a new family, if you will.

This is the lesson of Jesus trusting Mary to John's care.

> Standing by the cross of Jesus were his mother, his mother's sister, Mary the wife of Clopas, and Mary Magdalene. When Jesus saw his mother and the disciple he loved standing there, he said to his mother, "Woman, here is your son." Then he said to the disciple, "Here is your mother." And from that hour, the disciple took her into his home. (John 19:25–27)

Jesus, knowing that he is about to die, wants to ensure that his mother is cared for. She was a widow, and while his brothers would eventually become believers, at this time they were not yet followers of Christ. When Jesus entrusted his mom to his friend's care, he was making a statement on how we are to view family and the ties that bind. Is bloodline all that matters? In this moment, Jesus makes it clear that allegiance to the family of God supersedes the family tree.

In a culture where family bloodlines were everything, this is again a shocking departure from cultural norms. And let me just say, I *love* this about Jesus.

I grew up with a dad who was technically my stepdad, but we never used that term. In our family, he was my dad, the one who raised me as his own. For most of my life, he was the only father figure I had, and he was more than enough. There was nothing "less than" about his paternal role in my life. When my mom was pregnant with my brother, I heard the term "half-brother" from a meddlesome stick-in-the-mud. What a ridiculous thing! I could not wrap my thirteen-year-old brain around the idea. How could anyone be a half anything in a family? He was my brother. End of story.

Today, we have many people in our lives and our kids' lives—aunts and uncles who hold no blood relation but are every bit a part of our family. This is a tremendous blessing. If we kept the lines drawn solely around bloodlines, there would be very few people from my side of the family that my kids or I could truly call on. As we see Jesus demonstrate, though, adopting someone into your family is just as rich a connection, even richer, than the family ties that bind.

When Jesus commends his mother to John and John to her, he is showing us all what it looks like to be bonded in Christ. Even more so, it is a foreshadowing of the grafting into God's family that

Jesus's death makes a way for. The life, death, and resurrection of Jesus make a way for all to belong. How thankful I am for this truth!

In Christ, we experience an adoption into a family that is not based on our birthright or bloodline. We can also open ourselves to such a reality in our lives here on earth. The connectedness, the communion, that comes in Christian fellowship with those we do life with is designed to be that of familial living.

Do we hold space for that level of connectedness? Or do we solely hold that level of connectedness to the ones we are tied to through a bloodline? This moment on the cross is a call for us all to be more open in how we construct our families and experience a deeper connection than what we see modeled in the world. When we fully step into that, genuine joy reigns over our lives. The orphaned are not left alone. The widowed are comforted.

It is a strange thing to be an orphaned adult. In a way that is hard to express, I think you are more aware of the permanent need for family connections when they are removed from you as an adult. An adult does not require parents to provide food, shelter, or safety. As an adult, you might prefer to go without your parents' guidance, advice, and direction. The true void comes simply from the need to be a part of a family, to know that there are generations before you that love you simply for who you are. It is almost impossible to fulfill that particular need as an adult orphan. Almost.

My parents left us, myself and my siblings, a wonderful cabin tucked in the mountains on the edge of the most beautiful lake. We spent our childhood summers here. It was our haven—and it still is. What makes the lake so incredibly valuable is not just the stunning views, the beautiful creation, and the camp full of memories, but also our lake family.

There, gathered among a handful of cabins, we find the communal, connected family that we yearn for. There are generations of families that meet up each summer with strong ties and bonds.

It is hard to put into words what happens in that place. I believe the beginning and the end of it is an awareness of a connectedness that we do not, I do not, freely welcome in our everyday lives. We know each other's histories. We have borne witness to death and illness, to life and birth, to kids growing and adults aging. It is family as Jesus demonstrates.

Several years ago, our kids had a Grandparents' Day celebration at their school. It is a sweet event, with a brunch, chapel service, and visits to the classrooms, so students can show their grandparents what they have been working on in school. Before the event, my kids came to me and sheepishly asked if we could invite Grandma Linda and Grandpa Claude—our lake grandparents to attend the celebration at school. Linda and Claude have been in my life since I was five years old. I spent every childhood summer traipsing between their camp and ours, or spending the day at the beach in between the two. Linda and Claude, along with their kids, carry so many fond memories of my mom and my childhood. And they welcome my kids as if they were their own. It is a total delight to be in Grandma Linda's presence. Having someone who knows how you were raised, because they were *there*, is a great gift. Living so deeply entangled in one another's lives, even if only for six weeks of the year, creates deeper bonds than I can fully articulate.

But when my kids asked to invite them to Grandparents' Day, I hesitated. Was it appropriate? Was it assumptive? Had our pseudo-commune living set my kids up for disappointment? Eventually, I sheepishly approached Linda and offered the invitation. She responded with an immediate yes. This yes involved her taking a day off work, getting up and on the road by 5:00 a.m. to get to the kids' school on time, and driving several hours.

I was volunteering during the Grandparents' Day festivities and when I saw Linda and Claude walk through the doors, I burst into tears. I was completely taken aback by my emotions. I knew they had said yes, but I just couldn't believe they were there. As Grandma Linda hugged me tightly, she said, "Of course we would come. That is what family does." They spent the most beautiful day with the kids—loving them up in profound ways. I have never seen my kids act that attached or that connected, that assured of being loved wholly for exactly who they are and so proud to belong to someone. And although I can't speak for Linda or Claude, I know that our household continues to talk about their visit on that special day because it was just so beautiful.

I almost missed it. I almost robbed us of that display of what it looks like to be a family that the world might not quite understand.

The lesson of Jesus, Mary, and John is not just about how we define family but also about how we respond to the needs of those we are called to love or serve like family. I have had many opportunities to open our home, our family, to those who needed a safe, soft place to fall. I believe this is something we all can do. And to be honest, I didn't even feel stretched thin or run down in those circumstances. The individuals we have welcomed into our fold over the years were and are wonderful. And while I wouldn't trade these experiences for the world, it took Linda and Claude's beautiful gesture to make me truly understand the depth of formation that occurs when we serve and welcome others as if they are our own.

> Then he said to the disciple, "Here is your mother." And from that hour the disciple took her into his home. (John 19:27)

It is the response of John that changed Mary's future. He welcomed her into his home and cared for her as if she was his own. In my experience, having received such care from someone who treated me like family without the ties of a bloodline, I can attest to the impact of such a gesture—it changes things.

Mid-April 2020 found me at my dad's bedside after a sharp and relatively sudden decline in his health. We knew the end was imminent and close. We were in the any-day-now stage of end of life. It was an exhausting yet beautiful place to be. Simultaneously, my brother was across the country in California awaiting brain surgery. There was much discussion about when my brother should come home. A last-minute decision was made, an itinerary frantically sent as he raced to the airport to catch the first of three flights to get him home, hopefully in time to say goodbye to our dad. And thus began the longest night of my life.

In those weeks that led up to the final days, there were a handful of my dad's faithful lifelong friends that showed up and kept showing up every single day. It was an honor to sit with them, to hear the old familiar stories of their youths or young adulthoods, stories that even I knew well. Among them was an ex-girlfriend/childhood friend. Her kids spent a good amount of time with our family throughout the years, but she was more of a figure that, for me, existed in the past and had nothing to do with the family my dad had built. Their friendship carried on through the years in a way that honored the closeness of what it meant to truly grow up together. She interacted with my dad and only my dad, and they were loyal to each other in a way true friends are; yet she was mostly a stranger to me.

As the end drew near, I welcomed her support, particularly in scheduling hospital visits so that I could care for both my dad and my young family. We had pleasant, neutral exchanges as she or I would come and go, and that was about it. But then came the longest night.

Everyone was aware of the need to get my brother home safely to say goodbye. It seemed it would require a miracle to keep my dad alive long enough to make it all happen. We told my brother there was only a small chance our dad would be alive by the time he made it across the country, flight after connecting flight after connecting flight. But we knew it was something that we had to try to do. I alerted the group of my dad's friends that my brother, John, was on his way back from California and that I would be spending the night in the hospital praying my dad stayed alive to say goodbye to his son.

When I got to the hospice room that night, she was there, quietly waiting for me. Until this time, we had maintained a schedule of daytime shifts. We would pass along information and then head out the door as the other took their post at the bedside. By the time I had arrived on this, the longest night, it was already after 9 p.m. She said few words and gave almost no explanation for her presence other than she would not stand for me facing this night on my own. There was an assuredness about her that I knew to welcome, and so I sat down in one chair, she in another, and the longest night began. We spent that night curled up in hard hospital armchairs, trying to read, staring at the little airplane on my phone as I tracked John's flights across the country. Every few hours, I would say aloud where the plane was and that it had gained a few minutes of time, or alert her of the next layover that was particularly tight. Mainly, we just stared at my dad's chest, making sure he was still breathing, still with us, so that my brother would get his goodbye. (And yes, he did make it in time.)

There was not just a camaraderie but also a sense of my being cared for that was rather foreign to me. Having said goodbye to my mom long ago, I was used to being the elder of any crisis. I was the one that most often led the charge, stood in the gap, and cared for everyone else. But this night, I was not alone.

It was the most generous thing someone has ever done for me. I was seen as the orphan that I was and was becoming, and she stepped in that night, as a mother would, to come and sit alongside me. When I think of it, I am still undone. I had spent most of my adulthood without a parent; even when my dad was alive, he was not able to be a parent to me due to his numerous health conditions. But that night, I felt it: the one-sided, self-sacrificing love of family from someone I never expected.

If this concept of stepping in deeply outside of your biological family seems daunting to you, or if perhaps this was never modeled for you, or even if it is something you have felt uncomfortable with, I want to invite you to look once more at this moment on the cross. Jesus has something better for us than we imagine when we limit ourselves to considering family as something connected through blood or a genetic tie or even a family tree. May we welcome the deep connections that Christian community has for us.

Via Dolorosa Way of Grief

As we follow Jesus from Gethsemane to Golgotha and then to the tomb, take a few moments to sit quietly with him. Similar to the Way of the Cross or Stations of the Cross, we will pause to reflect on the moments and meaning of Good Friday. There is grief in death. But there is also grief in our sin and in our misalignment with God. Before we continue on, we must pause and grieve.

REFLECT

- What do you learn about family as you look at the cross?

- Where are you drawing relational lines?

- As you reflect, ask God to reveal his presence and will. What does he show you?

CONFESS

- Have you held too tightly to relationships?
- Have you closed yourself off?
- Where is there misalignment in your desires, actions, and thoughts?
- Where are you not valuing what Jesus valued?

RECONSIDER

- Letting go of our will and seeking God's will is the way to freedom, beauty, and life.
- The redemptive work begins with letting go of control.
- Take time to pray and affirm this.

CHAPTER TWELVE

IMPLAUSIBLE TIMING

Death of Presumptions

Jesus Dies without a Broken Bone | Jesus's Side Pierced

John 19:31–37

From a historic and scientific perspective, the timing of Jesus's death might seem nonsensical. Supernatural. You might not have spent much time pondering the time between when Jesus was crucified and when he died. Allow me to invite you into a sense of wondering about this. There is much to be learned as we contemplate the actual timing of Jesus's death.

I have found that timing is one of the things we work tightly to control. Our yearning for control can look like asserting what we think is best or demanding we know the schedule. Oftentimes it sounds like "Just tell me when" or "I would feel so much better if I just knew when this would be over" or "I don't mind waiting; I just want to know for how long I will be waiting." Control.

The death of Jesus on the cross, his actual death, can teach us a lot about this:

> Since it was the preparation day, the Jews did not want the bodies to remain on the cross on the Sabbath (for that Sabbath was a special day). They requested that Pilate have the men's legs broken and that their bodies be taken away. So the soldiers came and broke the legs of the first man and of the other one who had been crucified with him. When they came to Jesus, they did not break his legs since they saw that he was already dead. But one of the soldiers pierced his side with a spear, and at once blood and water came out. He who saw this has testified so that you also may believe. His testimony is true, and he knows he is telling the truth. For these things happened so that the Scripture would be fulfilled: Not one of his bones will be broken. Also, another Scripture says: They will look at the one they pierced. (John 19:31–37)

The details of this passage are brutal to read. Yet these verses have a purpose—beyond painting the grim picture of death by crucifixion. These gruesome details all point to a truth that we often miss: the timing of the death of Jesus was unpredictable within the earthly realm. These verses also serve to remind us of this fact: our own lives and deaths, and the timing of it all, are entirely unpredictable to man.

Jesus was crucified at noon, and he took his last breath just three hours later at 3:00 p.m. While the thought of our Savior in that kind of torturous, painful agony for three hours sounds excruciatingly long, the reality is, this was incredibly short in the world of Roman crucifixions. Shockingly so. The Romans had mastered the so-called art of crucifixion in that they had designed it in such a way that it caused the most drawn out means of torture as the victim perished. This process was designed to last as many as four days between the moment of crucifixion and the moment of death.[1] Yet here was Jesus, taking his last breath after only three hours.

Because of this timing, the Scriptures were fulfilled, and God's redeeming power was ultimately displayed.

With the high Sabbath of Passover coming at the end of the day, the Roman government, as a means of placating the Jewish leaders, was willing to handle the executions and subsequent removal of the bodies in an expeditious manner. Traditionally, after the several days it might take for a person to perish via crucifixion, the body was left hanging on the cross for days. This was yet another way for the Roman government to maximize the gruesomeness of such an execution. In deference to the Jewish custom that no dead body be left exposed and out in the open, the Roman government was willing to expedite any executions so that the bodies could be removed from the crosses. On any typical day, even a Sabbath day, the Jews would never approach the Roman government with the request to immediately take down and bury the body of an executed "criminal." But because this was a high Sabbath day, they proceeded differently. Timing is everything.

As a means of expediting the death, the Roman soldiers would break the legs of those crucified. This would cause several complications internally that would result in a speedy decline. This method was traditionally employed after a few days. But due to the holiday of Passover, the soldiers were prepared to move forward with this after just a few hours. Yet, when the soldiers approached Jesus, they realized it was not necessary—he was already gone.

Thus the Scriptures of the Passover lamb were ultimately fulfilled:

---

[1]F. P. Retief and L. Cilliers, "The History and Pathology of Crucifixion," *South African Medical Journal* 2003;93(12):938–41.

> It is to be eaten in one house. You may not take any of the meat outside the house, and you may not break any of its bones. (Exod. 12:46)

> They may not leave any of it until morning or break any of its bones. They must observe the Passover according to all its statutes. (Num. 9:12)

> He protects all his bones; not one of them will be broken. (Ps. 34:20 NIV)

At that point, the soldiers were unsure what to do. Jesus having already perished was implausible. So they confirmed Jesus's death by piercing his side and thus fulfilled more Scripture.

> But he was pierced for our transgressions, he was crushed for our iniquities; the punishment that brought us peace was on him, and by his wounds we are healed. (Isa. 53:5 NIV)

We know this verse in Isaiah points to the Messiah with beautiful, comforting prophecy. But we often miss that the fulfillment arose out of unexpected, unpredictable timing.

Had Jesus perished at a "normal" rate, the protocol of the day would have continued with him as it did with the other two criminals—legs broken, no need to pierce the side. But that is not what happened. We must look at the timing of what was used to bring about God's best, his full redemptive power. The timing of it all, *his* timing, was paramount. And while God himself knows the timing, we do not.

This lesson, for me, has played out many times, especially while waiting for a loved one to pass. If you have ever found yourself in a caregiving or hospice setting, then you know what I am talking about. I have sat with many hospice nurses who have graciously listened to my continued requests for updates: "How close are we?" If you have yet to interact with a member of a hospice team, let me assure you they are a very special group of people. These amazing nurses, chaplains, volunteers, and advocates are trained to walk alongside you and your loved ones as they pass away. And spending as much time in the presence of death as they do, the amazing people of hospice know this: attempting to predict death is foolish and arrogant. Yet we, the ones looking to control the uncontrollable, still want to know—*when*.

Our yearning for control and comfort in those wildly uncomfortable days of waiting on death never delivers what we desire. Truth be told, what I ultimately want, what I believe we all want, is God's best for us and our loved ones. Grappling for a schedule, trying to predict the timing, does not bring us closer to God's best.

I experienced this most profoundly in the almost simultaneous passing of my mom and the birth of our son.

About thirteen months after that night in the ER when we first discovered my mom's brain cancer, we now found ourselves at the end of her cancer battle. As her illness had progressed, we went through the standard protocol of treatment for glioblastoma, and when we exhausted that, we successfully pursued clinical trials. Then we exhausted that option as well. By April 2008, the end was near, and our options had run out. On top of all this, I was eight months pregnant. I was literally waiting on both life and death.

Mom was enrolled in hospice. We had biweekly visits from our amazing nurse. As she arrived for one of our visits, she found me in the guest room that Mom had occupied for the last six months, changing the sheets of her bed. By this point, my mom was not able to stand because her muscles had deteriorated so much. As I made her bed, she was not even able to roll over on her own. So, yes, she was in the bed while I changed the sheets. If you have ever cared for a patient like this, you know what this process entails. There is a way to lay the new sheets out, roll the patient from one side to the other, and then tuck in the new sheet all around. You can imagine how hard this is with a patient with no body control and a very pregnant caretaker. This is the scene our nurse walked into.

The nurse called me to the hallway and said to me, "It's time to talk about The Inn." The Inn is the hospice wing of our local hospital. They offer full-time, in-room hospice care. It is warm and lovely, quiet and serene. The problem was I didn't want my mom there yet. The Inn is usually a short-term stay, reserved for the last week or two, and that timing did not line up with what I had assumed we had. Yet it was clearly the right call by the nurse, for my mom and for me. Like it or not, the time was upon us.

So our family prepared for the relocation and the goodbye that would be coming in the next week or two. We spent hours there each day, enjoying the quiet and even a day of renewed energy that mom had. We thought we were right on track for our goodbye. So we waited. And we waited. Mom grew quiet again. She slept most of the day. And still we waited.

After two weeks, we began to get antsy. It felt as if we were waiting to jump off a cliff but hadn't yet been given the shove. Why couldn't someone just give us an accurate timeline of what to expect? After three weeks, we began to get frustrated. What is going on? How come this is taking so long? How come we are here at The Inn for so much longer than "usual"? After four weeks, we finally surrendered.

On Day 32, May 8, 2008, two days before my due date, I went to my weekly doctor's appointment. They announced what I already knew—no sign of the baby coming anytime soon. There had been no false labor, no dilation, nothing to show I was anywhere close to giving birth. I then waddled across the parking lot my doctor's office shared with the hospital and took the familiar route to The

Inn. I sat down next to my mom's bed and let out a huge sigh. I was frustrated.

She was mostly asleep, and even when she was awake, she was barely present. I will keep the exact words for her and me to hold, but in that moment, I called her out on the battle of wills we currently found ourselves in: she was holding on to life to see that grandbaby, and I was holding on to that grandbaby until I could let go of Mom. I told her I was surrendering it all and invited her to do the same. I acknowledged that this was not the way she wanted to experience her grandchildren, but it seemed that God had designed for her to see them from heaven. We had to lay down what we thought the timing was going to look like. I had no idea if she heard any of my words, but I left the hospital that afternoon with a peace that I had not experienced till then.

That was the day my mom passed away.

The next day, we finalized all the necessary arrangements. It was a day of running around and details, as those days tend to be. My last errand of the day was to pick up an embroidered canvas tote that I had selected as a diaper bag. It was a simple canvas bag from L.L.Bean, a favorite of our family, with the new baby's name on it, Maxson. I woke up the next morning, and as I got up from my bed, my water broke.

This was Saturday, May 10, my due date. The next day was Sunday, May 11, Mother's Day. And the following day was Monday, May 12, the day of the wake, with the funeral set for Tuesday. That string of dates was running through my brain at breakneck speed as I tried to sort out how I could possibly get through imminent labor and the waiting funeral services as I said, "No, no, no, no." Over and over again.

I found Josh and informed him of the new development. He was struck silent. I called my doctor, who agreed it was necessary to come to labor and delivery. Although it was a slow leak, it required me to come to the hospital ASAP. (Yes, I did ask if I really had to come in.) Then I began slowly moving through the house, figuring out how to tell the family what was going on. My sister happened upon me gathering items for my not-yet-packed hospital bag. "What's behind your back?" she asked. "Oh, nothing." She shot me a look and I instantly held up a series of items that could only point to one thing—the baby was coming. "You're kidding!" she exclaimed. But, no, I was not kidding.

I got settled in the hospital amid whispers of "Her mom just died" and "How awful" and "Poor thing." It was surreal. The attending doctor confirmed that my water had broken, and in an attempt to acknowledge the difficulty of the timing, said, "I am sorry to say your water has definitely broken." And with those few words, I was devastated. Not because of my water breaking but because of the sympathy and tragedy that was attached to this baby boy before he even arrived.

My body was in shock and wasn't allowing labor to come through, even though there was a tear in my placenta. We tried everything. The exercises, the meds, the food, the lack of food. Over the next forty-eight hours, we shifted between making all decisions with the goal of getting me to the funeral to then making all decisions as if this was a "normal" birth and then back and forth between the two. It was an exhausting rollercoaster of emotion. All the while, we acted as if we were in charge of what was happening and when. But the timing of life, just as death, is truly in God's hands.

Finally, we were released from the pretense of being in charge of when the baby would be born by an emergency C-section at 1:00 a.m. on Monday, May 12. Maxson was healthy and wonderful—full of life. We made it back to our room by 4:00 a.m., with just enough time for a nap before Josh had to leave at 8:00 a.m. to meet with our pastors to settle a few arrangements for the funeral.

While Josh was at church and back home gathering his clothes for the services, I came to terms with the reality that I was not going to be able to attend my mother's wake later that day. However, my amazing nurse, a true gift from God, plotted with me on a way to get to the funeral the next day. When she caught wind of my desire to "disappear for a few hours" the next day, she intervened, called a team meeting, and came up with an amazing, outlandish plan. If I could get up and walk a few steps today (yes, the same day as surgery), the team would set me up to go to the funeral, including letting me use a hospital wheelchair, keeping our newborn son in the hospital nursery while I attended, and encouraging me to discharge myself upon return from the funeral.

I got dressed in the hospital room for my mother's funeral the next morning. We left our newborn son in the nursery and made our way to say goodbye to Mom. The timing of it all seemed so implausible. How could this be God's best for us?

After the service and the burial, as the luncheon was winding down, I looked around the room at the people who knew Mom and loved her, who loved our whole family. It was such a sweet vision of life carrying on. I looked at Josh and said, "Let's go get our baby." And with that, we returned to the hospital, picked up that perfect baby boy, and went home. We brought him into the house, set his infant carrier on the floor next to my dad, and all took a deep exhale.

During those few days, life and death intertwined in beautiful, painful ways. What I know now is that God's timing during those trying days saved me in profound ways. If Max had arrived at any other time, I would have been lost. That little baby showed us that God had good things in store for us. That while there would be trials and even death, there also would be joy and life. Both at the same time. We had just experienced both simultaneously.

I never would have hoped or even known to ask for the timing of Mom's death and Max's birth to be so entwined. But that is how it goes with God's timing. We don't ever really know the reason when we are caught up in the moment. However, when we look back, we see God's goodness and mercy, his redemptive power on display. Just as it was on Good Friday.

May we find comfort in accepting that there is no comfort in our predictions of any timeline, but instead welcome the unbelievable, often implausible timing that comes from God and leads us to his best for us.

Via Dolorosa Way of Grief

As we follow Jesus from Gethsemane to Golgotha and then to the tomb, take a few moments to sit quietly with him. Similar to the Way of the Cross or Stations of the Cross, we will pause to reflect on the moments and meaning of Good Friday. There is grief in death. But there is also grief in our sin and in our misalignment with God. Before we continue on, we must pause and grieve.

REFLECT

- What do you notice about the timing of the day of Good Friday?

- Where do you see something unexpected happening?

- As you reflect, ask God to reveal his presence and will. What does he show you?

CONFESS

- Do you welcome God's control of your schedule?
- Do you assume you know the timeline?
- Where is there misalignment in your desires, actions, and thoughts?
- Where are you not valuing what Jesus valued?

RECONSIDER

- Letting go of our will and seeking God's will is the way to freedom, beauty, and life.
- The redemptive work begins with letting go of control.
- Take time to pray and affirm this.

CHAPTER THIRTEEN

UPENDING TRADITIONS

Death of How It Was

The Curtain Rips

Matthew 27:50–51 | Mark 15:37–38 | Luke 23:45

Traditions matter. They ground us when we feel untethered. As Tevye from *Fiddler on the Roof* would remind us, "Tradition!" is a call unto itself. In the keeping of tradition, we keep ourselves connected. In a world where we are all adrift more than ever right now, it can be good to lean into traditions. Traditions remind us of who we are, whose we are, and where we came from. They can be beautiful.

I come from a family wrought with traditions. And, yes, we loved the song from *Fiddler* and would sing it loud and proud whenever possible. Knowing now how much of my life would be spent without my parents, I am very thankful for the traditions I grew up with as a means of connecting my kids to the generations that came before. It connects me to them as well.

If we are not careful, though, we can take a tradition and elevate it to the place of an idol. It happens more subtly than you might think. Where there was once true connection, there can be instead an empty ceremony. Where there was once deep meaning, there can be instead a shallow performance.

Holding too tightly to traditions can prevent us from welcoming a new way of doing things, a new way to connect. This is why we must hold even our traditions in a posture of surrender. Our desire to control what we do and insistence on doing it the way it has always been done can be the very thing blocking an even better way for us. We come face-to-face with this reality in the moment when Jesus takes his last breath and God shows, in a glorious way, that something new is happening:

> But Jesus cried out again with a loud voice and gave up his spirit. Suddenly, the curtain of the sanctuary was torn in two from top to bottom, the earth quaked, and the rocks were split. (Matt. 27:50–51)

This curtain, also known as the veil, was an incredible masterpiece of craftsmanship. It was approximately sixty feet high and twenty feet wide. There is much scholarly work on the thickness of the curtain. The majority view is that it was the thickness of a hand, measuring approximately four inches thick. Intricately woven, as described in Exodus and 2 Chronicles, the curtain was likely woven on a loom with seventy-two rods, and over each rod were twenty-four threads. Even more astounding was how heavy it was! Ancient Jewish texts from the Mishnah report that cleaning the curtain would require the labor of three hundred priests just to lift it![1]

[1]Daniel M. Gurtner, "The Veil of the Temple in History and Legend," *Journal of the Evangelical Theological Society*, March 2006, https://www.etsjets.org/files/JETS-PDFs/49/49-1/JETS_49-1_97-114_Gurtner.pdf.

This was a beautiful, valuable, and sizable tapestry. Nevertheless, the most important thing about the veil was its purpose. It was used as a way to fully block the innermost part of the temple, called the holy of holies. This was based on the very explicit plans for the tabernacle in Exodus, carried over to Solomon's temple and then replicated in the rebuilt temple of Jesus's time, known as Herod's temple.

The holy of holies originally held the ark of the covenant, the dwelling place of God. Once a year, on Yom Kippur (the Day of Atonement), the high priest would go into the holy of holies to offer a sacrifice. This was established in Leviticus 16 and carried on throughout the years. During the time of Jesus's death, the holy of holies no longer held the ark of the covenant, since it had been lost in battle, yet it was still the most sacred place, blocked off from all other parts of the temple. The curtain was literally the barrier between communion with God and all of humanity.

This is why the moment of its tearing was so monumental. Matthew, Mark, and Luke all include an account of it ripping from top to bottom at the exact moment of Jesus's death. The ripping alone was amazing. The ancient texts describe that oxen or horses tied to each corner of the curtain could not rip it.[2] It was not something that could simply unravel, even at will. Further, the tear was from top to bottom. The top of the curtain was more than ten stories high. This was an act of God and occurred in such a way as to leave no room for being identified as anything other than that.

The barrier was ripped. Suddenly, there was full access to God.

We see this as a glorious reality that we live in every single day. Of course we have full access to God! At the time, though, this was unfathomable. The curtain had been established with the building of the tabernacle and painstakingly upheld. This was tradition. This

[2]Gurtner, "The Veil of the Temple in History and Legend."

was how the people of God interacted with him. Through the high priest, only able to be in the presence of God, once a year, on the Day of Atonement to offer sacrifice. This and only this. Tradition.

But the tradition was just upended for something far better.

In the death of Jesus Christ, we find the ultimate sacrifice. And in that, we find the barrier removed between us and God. Full access. There is a new and better way to commune with God. More intimacy, more meaning. The veil is torn.

Interestingly, there were extra veils available at the temple. The ancient Jewish texts indicate that it took about six months to make a single veil, and it seems like they were always in production. I find this fascinating because it leads me to believe that the ripped curtain, the one that was torn on Good Friday, was easily replaced with an intact curtain. Seemingly it was, as there are continued accounts of the veil of the temple hanging in front of the holy of holies, intact, until its destruction at the hands of Titus in AD 70.

Take a moment and consider that. A curtain, over ten stories high, a handsbreadth thick, miraculously is ripped from top to bottom at the moment Jesus Christ dies. And rather than accept that God has, with total authority, upended the barrier between himself and all people, there was a choice made to pull down the ripped veil and replace it once again with the barrier as it had been.

This begs the question, how tightly are we holding on to tradition? If the ripped veil was replaced with an intact veil, does it not show the human inclination to hang on to what was, even when shown something better? How easy is it for us, today, to hang on to what we have always done as well?

Living through all the changes of the COVID-19 pandemic has brought this into a new light for me. Many traditions were upended during the height of the pandemic: family gatherings reimagined, schooling reinterpreted, in-person connections severed, church attended virtually, holidays in isolation—the list goes on. There was so much change as we did the best we could with what was available. But I also believe there was, amid it all, some upending that was good for us.

I am a huge believer in the power of community and connection. Friendship was important to Jesus, so friendship is important to me. I also know firsthand that true connection takes time, face-to-face. I was a vocal basher of using screens as a substitute for true connection. However, in the middle of a pandemic, how do we find ways to connect meaningfully? The whole world was going virtual.

How do you respond when the way you have done things is no longer available to you? The COVID-19 pandemic offered us a crash course in reimagining our traditions. This reimagining helped us strip off the superfluous and focus on the essential. We were forced to reckon with questions: What was church? What parts were we willing to let go of, and what parts were critical to hold on to? Is it possible to have a joyous holiday celebration with just the immediate family residing in your own home? Are you willing to connect via an app when it is the only way to do so? Are screens only detrimental to your relationship, or is there a way to authentically show up virtually?

As I write this, we are hopefully on our way out of the pandemic. There is much talk about returning to normal. I wonder what we will take with us from this experience as we shift back into some semblance of normalcy. Will we be grasping for how it was?

The biggest shift for me, as I imagine for most of us, has been the increased use of video conferencing. While I do know most of us are "Zoomed out" by this point (myself included), I do see how my embrace of technology has changed a few key areas of my life in profound ways. I would not have asked to change these parts of my life, but I can now see how change is a gift—and one I intend to hold on to.

I have already shared about the very special community we have at our cabin. For my entire childhood, they were my people. But only my summer people. Each year around Columbus Day, we would say goodbye for the year. And then each Memorial Day weekend, we would meet again. We kids would slowly creep out of our respective cabins and meander down to the collective drive where we would ever so slowly and sheepishly make our way to each other to rekindle our sacred friendships once again. After a few quiet moments and awkward silences, we would find our way and within ten minutes, we would be back to where we left off and the cycle would begin again.

Once I became a mom, I would look out the door of the cabin and watch this sweet ritual play out with our kids, the next generation. The nudging of the kids to head down to the drive to say hello to their buddies, the awkward quiet, and then the return to the rhythm of friendship and camaraderie. There was comfort found in knowing that this special place was trapped in time, that traditions carry on.

But then we encountered the world reimagined through COVID-19. As we prepared to say our annual goodbyes in the autumn of 2020, we moms realized that with virtual school and homeschool, we could continue to meet at the lake through the beginning of the school year. It felt strange, but it was like a gift offered to us in a season of much loss and confusion. Our kids became more attached to each other than ever before.

Once we settled into life away from the lake in the COVID world, I realized that my kids, yearning for connection, found great delight in spending time on Zoom with their friends. Zoom had become every adult's nemesis—a means to get work done. But for the kids, it was only a positive and fun association. So I began to set up times for them to connect with the peers they normally would have connected with during the school year.

Then they approached me and asked if they could Zoom with Ryan and Emma. Ryan and Emma? But they were lake friends. They were summer friends. This was not summer and we were not at the lake. If we connect with them now, what will happen to the rhythm of the reunion and the goodbye? What will happen to how things have always been?

Realizing what a poor argument that was and wanting to grab as much joy as we could in that unprecedented time, I relented. Albeit begrudgingly. Oh, if only I knew that what would come from my willingness to release a tradition ended up being a true highlight of our pandemic season, I would never have hesitated. Because when we list out the gifts of this time, high on the list are the times the kids connected with Ryan and Emma over video. They have worked on designing video games, sewing innumerable projects, and showing each other their bedrooms at home, with true year-round friendship moments, all from my welcoming the use of screens and my willingness to let go of one small tradition in favor of a much better thing.

As I write it out it seems so obvious, of course. My kids now have year-round access to their lake friendships, but the weight of my summer tradition was so heavy that I believed there was only one way. What I learned instead is that sometimes we have an improvement or change available to us, one that we would likely have never chosen but is chosen for us. May we say yes when given the chance.

The beauty of the reinvention we see on Good Friday is that it paved the way for something better, far better than we could have imagined. This is how we know it is time to let go of a tradition. When the tradition unnecessarily blocks us from intimacy with God, it is time to rip it up. I believe the same measures can be applied to our own traditions. If it holds more pomp and circumstance than richness; if it impedes authentic community, then it is time to reinvent. May we welcome the upending of our traditions, trusting God to bring us that much closer to him and to each other.

Via Dolorosa Way of Grief

As we follow Jesus from Gethsemane to Golgotha and then to the tomb, take a few moments to sit quietly with him. Similar to the Way of the Cross or Stations of the Cross, we will pause to reflect on the moments and meaning of Good Friday. There is grief in death. But there is also grief in our sin and in our misalignment with God. Before we continue on, we must pause and grieve.

REFLECT

- What do you observe in the reinvention of tradition on Good Friday?

- What traditions do you hold tightly?

- As you reflect, ask God to reveal his presence and will. What does he show you?

CONFESS

- Have you turned a tradition into an empty ceremony?
- Have you blocked the way for greater intimacy?
- Where is there misalignment in your desires, actions, and thoughts?
- Where are you not valuing what Jesus valued?

RECONSIDER

- Letting go of our will and seeking God's will is the way to freedom, beauty, and life.
- The redemptive work begins with letting go of control.
- Take time to pray and affirm this.

PART FOUR

Beauty for Ashes

As we witness the death of Jesus, we are left with the question, "What now?" The Lord in his faithfulness shows us how we can trade the ashes of grief and mourning for beauty by living a life surrendered. We get to experience the beauty of certainty, boldness, and freedom from fear.

CHAPTER FOURTEEN

CERTAINTY

Death of Doubt

Soldier Declares Jesus the Son of God

Matthew 27:54 | Mark 15:39 | Luke 23:47

Some of the most beautiful moments of my life have been when heaven breaks through. Have you ever experienced it? I have had the joy of watching a butterfly land on the foot of a grieving mother; a cardinal, or ten, inexplicably show up outside a window; a truly glorious sunset radiate in a special way. I have been on my paddleboard on a lake as still as glass when suddenly, seemingly out of nowhere, a breeze picked up and I could truly feel, deep within my soul, something special was happening. Breakthrough.

The breaking through of heaven is a gift. Some may experience it several times throughout their lives, but it is the *first* time that truly changes everything. That is the moment when doubt fades away and certainty settles in.

I love the word "truly." I love that Jesus used the word truly in conversation often. "Truly, I say to you" is a phrase we hear him use over and over. I think it speaks to the fact that Jesus was always pointing to the truth, the truth of the Word, the truth of the Father, the truth of himself. And to the certainty found in that truth.

When my dad would be in a particularly silly or sentimental mood, he would say to me, "I love you, truly." He would then burst into song, a squeaky rendition of Perry Como singing, "I love you truly, truly dear." There was such sincerity in those squeaky words. That is what "truly" points us to. "Truly" is something you can trust.

This certainty is present at the cross. As Jesus drew his last breath, the curtain ripped open. Some scholars say, in addition to the very real ripping of the curtain, it was also a metaphor for the tearing open of heaven itself. Breakthrough. The response of the centurion, the commander of the Roman army charged with watching over the crucifixion, was one of shock. He witnessed the breakthrough and, suddenly, doubt fled.

> When the centurion, who was standing opposite him, saw the way he breathed his last, he said, "Truly this man was the Son of God!" (Mark 15:39)

This Roman soldier was the first to recognize the true identity of Jesus in response to his death. He had mocked Jesus just moments before, casting lots for his garment. He was the commander of the execution and crucifixion. If he didn't directly nail Jesus to the cross, he ordered the deed to be done. And surely he laughed with the others at the title hanging above Christ's head: "King of the Jews."

But then heaven broke through.

The curtain ripped. Jesus cried out in his last breath, "It is finished" (John 19:30), in such a way that the centurion standing opposite him knew, without any doubt. "Truly this man was the Son of God!" (Mark 15:39).

Earlier in Jesus's ministry, there had been moments of breakthrough, where he displayed the full power of God. In particular, when Jesus walked on the water, we see the cost of doubt and then the certainty that comes when doubt is destroyed:

> "Come," he said. Then Peter got down out of the boat, walked on the water and came toward Jesus. But when he saw the wind, he was afraid and, beginning to sink, cried out, "Lord, save me!" Immediately Jesus reached out his hand and caught him. "You of little faith," he said, "why did you doubt?" And when they climbed into the boat, the wind died down. Then those who were in the boat worshiped him, saying, "Truly you are the Son of God." (Matt. 14:29–33 NIV)

Jesus asks Peter, "Why did you doubt?" As Peter collects himself and he and Jesus climb back into the boat, the others realize and confess, "Truly you are the Son of God." They proclaim what is certain. And with that proclamation, doubt flees.

I often find comfort in Peter's shortcomings. There he is, walking across the water to Jesus, yet doubt creeps in. Oh, Peter. Those moments of doubt are ones I know as well. We all do. Notice that Jesus does not condemn him at the moment of his doubt, but rather asks him a question. "Why?" This is critical. Jesus is asking Peter, then, and us today, to hold open even our doubt to him. It is an invitation to consider, rather than an admonishment.

Will you give him even your doubt?

My dad was an agnostic for most of his adult life. He was of the mindset, "I want to have faith; just show me the proof first." Perhaps this was the result of an early faith built on empty ceremony more than true communion. Maybe it was the result of his career in law enforcement and government investigating and seeking facts. Perhaps, and most likely, this was the result of misplaced doubt. He grew up with no room for questions and grew into a person that demanded concrete answers. Neither are good places to be when seeking faith.

In response to my faith, he would often ask me, "But how do you know?" I would explain to him how I came to my own conclusions. I would explain to him that faith is being sure of that which you cannot see. Faith based on facts is hardly faith at all. His response was always along the lines of "It's possible . . . but . . . ." Always specific in claiming to be agnostic *not* atheist, he would clarify that he thought it suspect that anyone could claim they knew what is impossible to actually know. Yet he was always asking me about the confidence I had in my faith. In those questions he began to release the grip around his doubt and hold it more loosely. It was knowing he could voice the questions without causing upset or offense that truly began to offer him a place to change the posture of his doubt, to hold it more openly.

Fast-forward to the days before his death. He was in a nursing rehab hospital while enrolled in hospice. (His journey, as I've noted, was a complicated and swift decline.) I was spending several hours a day with him. Most nights, I would be home for dinner and tucking my kids in. It was one of those nights, another day in our new normal, when I had made it home in time for dinner and bed. I was just settling in when a nagging feeling came over me and would not let go. I had to go back to see my dad. I tried to ignore it. I tried to shake it. It would not cease. Finally, I told Josh I was heading back to sit by my dad for a bit. I grabbed a book and headed out the door.

When I arrived around 9:30 p.m., he was sleeping peacefully. I sat down next to him, he grabbed my hand, and I began to read to myself. We sat that way for half an hour or so. Me, reading to myself; him, staring off straight ahead, awake yet quiet. Then he let go of my hand and started speaking:

"It's not that door."

"What?" I asked.

"I can open the door. But I want to open that other door."

He continued saying some version of this several times. I tried to ease his worry. I tried to distract him. To no avail.

"I can't open the other door," he insisted.

Finally, I offered, "When I am not sure what to do, I pray. Do you think we should talk to Jesus about this?"

"Yes," he said as he let out a sigh filled with peace. And so as he patted my hand, I stood next to him and prayed aloud. We asked Jesus to guide him, asked for help opening the door, admitting that we believed Jesus was the one who could do it for my dad.

"Good," was his response as he once again patted my hand.

I sat back down, shaken.

"You look like her," he began.

"Who?"

"Her. The one standing next to you and next to the door."

As I am sure you deducted, there was no one there that I could see. Thoughts began to race. What was he seeing? Who was he seeing? Based on the next few things he said, it became clear to me that he was seeing my mom, who had passed away twelve years earlier.

To this day, I have more questions than answers about this encounter. I know for certain the Spirit prompted me to get up off my couch at home, get back in my car, and drive over there. My dad, who had lived his adult life as a doubter, was given a glimpse of two doors, and he knew for certain which door he wanted to open. He was anxious and upset, unsettled. Then we prayed and asked for Jesus's intervention and direction in his life, and there was suddenly peace, an open door, and my mom.

Heaven broke through that night. The doubt was relinquished. I was in the room when this happened, and it has taken me years to even be able to write about it, to share about it. It feels at once too far-fetched and too certain to be so. Yet it is.

Something happens when we offer our doubt to God with open hands. We are able to connect with the Spirit in a way that will transform us. It allows us to witness the breakthrough for what it is: a move of God designed to eradicate doubt. Surrendering his doubt is perhaps the greatest thing my dad ever did. It caused him to tremble. It caused him to seek the one with the answers.

Do not be afraid of doubt. Offer it to God and look for the breakthrough. Truly, I tell you, it will come.

Via Dolorosa Way of Grief

As we follow Jesus from Gethsemane to Golgotha and then to the tomb, take a few moments to sit quietly with him. Similar to the Way of the Cross or Stations of the Cross, we will pause to reflect on the moments and meaning of Good Friday. There is grief in death. But there is also grief in our sin and in our misalignment with God. Before we continue on, we must pause and grieve.

REFLECT

- What does the cross show us about doubt?

- Where are you experiencing doubt?

- As you reflect, ask God to reveal his presence and will. What does he show you?

CONFESS

- Have you held your doubt with an open hand?

- Have you looked for the breakthroughs of heaven?

- Where is there misalignment in your desires, actions, and thoughts?

- Where are you not valuing what Jesus valued?

RECONSIDER

- Letting go of our will and seeking God's will is the way to freedom, beauty, and life.
- The redemptive work begins with letting go of control.
- Take time to pray and affirm this.

CHAPTER FIFTEEN

BOLDNESS

Death of Fear

Joseph Buries Jesus's Body

Matthew 27:57–60 | Mark 15:42–46 | Luke 23:50–53 | John 19:38–40

After Jesus died, there was only a short window of time left in the day before the Sabbath began. This is important to note because what happened next required swift, bold thinking and action. We find such things in a man named Joseph:

> There was a good and righteous man named Joseph, a member of the Sanhedrin, who had not agreed with their plan and action. He was from Arimathea, a Judean town, and was looking forward to the kingdom of God. He approached Pilate and asked for Jesus's body. Taking it down, he wrapped it in fine linen and placed it in a tomb cut into the rock, where no one had ever been placed. (Luke 23:50–53)

This is one of those moments in the course of Good Friday that we can easily take for granted. Of course, familiar with the events of the day, we know Jesus was laid in Joseph's tomb. It is, after all, the tomb he will gloriously rise from in just a few days. But to truly understand the courage it took, we must slow down and look at Joseph. He is an amazing example of what happens when we are no longer afraid of being recognized as a disciple of Jesus.

As we stated earlier, due to the high holy day of the Passover Sabbath, the bodies of the crucified were permitted to be removed from the crosses rather than left there indefinitely. However, Jewish law held that such criminals' bodies would be placed in a mass grave. Even further, it was forbidden to publicly mourn for someone convicted of treason (like Jesus). The only exception to this would be if someone of high stature intervened on the convicted person's behalf.

In other words, were it not for Joseph's intervention, there would be no tomb at all.

Joseph was, according to Mark 15:43, a prominent member of the Sanhedrin. Matthew 27:57 describes him as a wealthy man. In this world of power, Joseph surely had plenty. His clout is confirmed when considering Pilate took a meeting with him outside his public hours. Public hours concluded at noon. When Joseph called upon Pilate, he answered. This is no small thing. While it is not specified, I am led to believe that Joseph was a Sadducee. The Sadducees, more so than the Pharisees, were wealthy and tended to be more elite. They were also the louder opponents of Christ in the trials earlier that day.[1]

---

[1]There is no scriptural reference to Joseph being a Sadducee. But based on his wealth (evident by his owning of the tomb) and the minimal information (the Sadducees did not continue after AD 70, which was the fall of Jerusalem and the loss of a great many records), I have concluded it is quite possible he was a Sadducee. Had he been a Pharisee, he would likely not have had the wealth needed to own a tomb and would have been mentioned in the post-AD 70 records, as the Pharisees continued after the fall of Jerusalem.

All four Gospels agree that Joseph was not just a rich member of the Sanhedrin but also already a disciple of Jesus. Joseph did not agree with the dealings of the day. He is described as good and righteous—one who looked forward to the kingdom of God rather than worked against it. Yet there is no recording of his objections. There is no mention of him as doing anything other than secretly following Jesus—until he boldly approached Pilate. In one fell swoop, Joseph not only outed himself as a follower of Jesus but also willingly spent all his political collateral to break Jewish law and ensure Jesus had a proper burial.

In making such a request to Pilate, Joseph puts himself in danger with Rome and with the Sanhedrin—the two powers responsible for the execution. Yet, with a freedom that comes from having no fear, Joseph is more concerned about what it means to be a true follower of Jesus than he is of others' perceptions or the personal consequences that could result. It is a truly astonishing shift that occurs within the span of this one day.

In the early days of our life together, Josh worked at a small jewelry store in a sleepy little town. It was run by a wonderful family who welcomed Josh and me as one of their own. Attached to the jewelry store was the family's clothing store. Our friend Ali ran the clothing store, and his wife Lisa worked there. Ali was raised Muslim, and Lisa was raised Jewish. Right after our wedding, Josh and I settled into a small church in town. Right around the same time, Ali started asking Josh some questions about the Christian faith. And it came to pass, within a year or two of those first conversations, that Lisa and Ali both gave their lives to Jesus.

Josh and I rejoiced when we heard the news. By this time, we had relocated to care for my mom and family. About a year or so later, I was driving through town and stopped to say hello to their family. Lisa was at the jewelry store, and she and I had a hushed conversation in the front of the store that I have never forgotten. She spoke about how transformed her entire life felt. She also shared about navigating her new faith, especially with some extended family members who held very different viewpoints. There was a tentativeness about it that broke my heart. I remember saying to her that if she held fast, there would come a time when she and Ali would be so sure and steady in their faith, so free, that a certain boldness would come. Soon they would no longer feel burdened by the response of others and would be living out their faith with confidence.

And that is exactly what happened. We would hear about the small groups they were running for teens, retreats they were a part of, Bible studies they led, and the like. It was encouraging to see our friends continuing to step into their faith. Then, two years ago, a decade after that hushed conversation, things changed for their family in dramatic ways. Their teenage daughter was hit by a car in a tragic accident. They were desperate as their daughter's life hung in the balance and held prayer sessions for her recovery every single night at 9:00 p.m. These calls to prayer were shared literally all over the world. My favorite moment during this trying yet inspiring time was when prayer groups started to gather in front of the family's store. While Lisa and Ali were with their daughter in the hospital several hours away, there were people praying on the sidewalk in front of the family store. God worked, and continues to work, miracles upon miracles in their family. Soon enough, people began to notice. Lisa's family was interviewed for the paper, boldly proclaiming the name of Jesus Christ. Soon after, Lisa started to make daily social media posts about the sustaining power of Jesus. In so doing, she began changing others' lives, sharing about the steadiness of Jesus in the middle of their family's trials.

Boldness came. Lisa and her family had experienced the freedom of living out from under the burden of others' reactions. There was no fear in being known as a disciple of Jesus. And this is exactly what we see from Joseph as he and Nicodemus bury Jesus in the tomb.

> After this, Joseph of Arimathea, who was a disciple of Jesus—but secretly because of his fear of the Jews—asked Pilate that he might remove Jesus's body. Pilate gave him permission; so he came and took his body away. Nicodemus (who had previously come to him at night) also came, bringing a mixture of about seventy-five pounds of myrrh and aloes. They took Jesus's body and wrapped it in linen cloths with the fragrant spices, according to the burial custom of the Jews. (John 19:38–40)

I love this picture of the two men, a Pharisee and a Sadducee, working together to break protocol and ensure the Son of God is honored properly. I wonder how they connected.[2] The Great Sanhedrin was composed of seventy men. Did they have secret meetings to discuss Jesus? Surely Nicodemus had an amazing encounter (as we see in John 3:1–21) to share about after having spent time with Jesus. Perhaps Joseph had heard of this and wanted to learn more. It is interesting to think about as we consider what led these two men to the tomb as the sun was setting and Sabbath was quickly approaching. Certainly, it was at that moment that their willingness to be known as disciples emboldened them to

[2]It is confirmed in Scripture that Nicodemus was a Pharisee, which makes it that much more interesting to consider that Joseph may have been a competing member of the Sanhedrin: a Sadducee. This would make the union of these two men, working together, all the more amazing. It sets forth a vision of unity possible when following Christ.

come with seventy pounds of oil and resin to prepare the body of Jesus.

They resisted the urge to let the opinions of others, even those within the religious power structure, hold them back from doing what was needed to honor their faith.

This is what we must continue to press toward. We must look for the other followers in our lives and embolden them. How much braver and fortified did Joseph feel having Nicodemus by his side as they laid the body of Jesus in the tomb?

When we step out of the shadows and boldly claim our place as a follower of Jesus, we may just find ourselves on a holy assignment. I had such an experience and it changed the way I approach other believers.

Waiting outside the ballet studio for my daughter to finish her rehearsal, I was . . . grumpy. As usual. I was aware of being surrounded by what I perceived as catty, superficial women who seemed to always get hung up on gossip and materialism. Not pretty—and I am referring to my attitude here. As I sat there stewing in my judgment and condemnation, right around the corner was a group of women talking about praying for their kids. Nothing catty, materialistic, or judgmental going on here.

I had been coming to rehearsal for weeks and had never paid attention to what was going on, beyond the handful of people I was immediately surrounded with. When I finally started looking up and paying attention to the folks around me, I started catching little pieces of their conversations. The next week at practice, I decided to sit closer to the group. When one mom started talking about how she was praying with her kids, I admitted that I did that too. "You do? Oh, thank goodness." Relief. Encouragement. And boldness. We spent the next few weeks getting to know each other and encouraging each other. We talked about Jesus and school and raising kids. It was all so refreshing and encouraging.

When I was invited to a birthday party of someone in the group, I was told the family was asking for donations to a charity that helps families who have a child with a terminal illness. It was a foundation I had worked with for years. I was curious about their connection. When I arrived at the studio the next week, I asked about the foundation and was shocked to know that the mom who was eight months pregnant was planning on using the foundation's help for their yet unborn son. The very foundation that I assisted with.

I was able to step in and help the family with arrangements after the baby's passing and as they honored him the next year on the anniversary of his passing. The family expressed that I was exactly who they needed at that time. And to think that I had almost missed my assignment from God to help this family. All because I was being closed off instead of bold in my faith.

I vowed to never again shy away from the delight it is to be a person who lives in a way the world doesn't understand. To not let bitterness take root when confronted with a hostile environment. To instead press in, ask God where the other disciples are, and boldly step into the assignments he has for me.

May we welcome the assignments God has for us, the ones that require boldness but lead to freedom.

Via Dolorosa Way of Grief

As we follow Jesus from Gethsemane to Golgotha and then to the tomb, take a few moments to sit quietly with him. Similar to the Way of the Cross or Stations of the Cross, we will pause to reflect on the moments and meaning of Good Friday. There is grief in death. But there is also grief in our sin and in our misalignment with God. Before we continue on, we must pause and grieve.

REFLECT

- What boldness do you see on Good Friday?
- Are you experiencing the freedom of boldness?
- As you reflect, ask God to reveal his presence and will. What does he show you?

CONFESS

- Have you shied away from being known as a disciple?
- What will it take to step into that freedom?
- Where is there misalignment in your desires, actions, and thoughts?

- Where are you not valuing what Jesus valued?

RECONSIDER

- Letting go of our will and seeking God's will is the way to freedom, beauty, and life.
- The redemptive work begins with letting go of control.
- Take time to pray and affirm this.

CHAPTER SIXTEEN

FEARLESS

Death of the Fear of Death

The Women Face the Tomb

Matthew 27:55–56, 61 | Mark 15:40–41, 47 | Luke 23:49, 55

The women stayed. The women stayed until the end. It was their unwillingness to look away from the cross that ultimately led them to the resurrection.

As Jesus hung on the cross; as he spoke his last words and took his last breath; as the darkness covered the sky and the curtain ripped—the women did not leave. Even more than that, they did not look away. When there was nothing to do, no way to stop the pain or suffering, no way to prevent what was happening, they held their ground and bore witness. They faced death.

> Many women who had followed Jesus from Galilee and looked after him were there, watching from a distance. Among them were Mary Magdalene, Mary the mother of James and Joseph, and the mother of Zebedee's sons. (Matt. 27:55–56)

> There were also women watching from a distance. Among them were Mary Magdalene, Mary the mother of James the younger and of Joses, and Salome. In Galilee these women followed him and took care of him. Many other women had come up with him to Jerusalem. (Mark 15:40–41)

I believe women are supernaturally equipped to face death in a way that men are not. There is a deep-rooted connection between being someone capable of carrying new life and the willingness to also face death. Life and death are so intricately tied together.

In my mom's last weeks, while she was at The Inn, I learned that many of the hospice nurses previously had been labor and delivery nurses, and many of the labor and delivery nurses previously had been in hospice! They view the two positions as almost interchangeable: life and death. The nurses affirmed that both roles require the same type of care—welcoming life and welcoming death.

In those days when life and death were so entwined for my family, where we said goodbye to Mom and hello to Max, I felt it deeply as well. Understanding the undeniable connection between life and death has helped me immensely when I have been called again and again to bear witness.

Watching someone die is incredibly difficult. I am not referring specifically to the last moments but rather the last days and weeks. But bearing witness requires us to show up. To see them struggling for breath, the caving in of their cheeks, the changes of their skin color. It is an act of bravery. It requires our fearlessness—being fearless enough to face death.

We are all offered the option to show up or wait for death to pass. I have never regretted a single moment of showing up. Remember, the women at the cross said nothing; they simply were present. This is all that is asked of us as well. It is in the showing up that we bless our friends or family. It is in the showing up that we are ourselves formed by Christ.

God has offered me many opportunities to practice a relative sense of comfort and peace in the face of death, having seen life and death together for so many years. Our family has lost many and almost lost even more. I know the inside of an ICU, ER, rehab, nursing home, hospice, hospital room, SICU, infusion room—and the list goes on. Familiarity does breed comfort.

But comfort is not what we are after. Instead, we seek a fearlessness that allows us to bear witness to the death around us—to step into the reality that life leads to death. When we surrender our lives at the foot of the cross, we welcome the truth of death. Rather than fear, there is confidence. Faith over fear.

If we are able to live this out with death around us, then I believe we will be far better equipped to handle the death within us. When it is our time to face death, we will be equipped to do so with fearlessness.

It was a usual evening in what had become our typical days of caregiving for Mom—working through appointments; giving treatments; and making sure she ate, drank, and rested, as required by her care regimen. She was well enough to move about the house and was still able to talk to us, albeit often struggling to connect the words in her brain and articulate. This was perhaps the greatest challenge of her diagnosis. She was not just a cancer patient; she was also a brain injury patient. She was not our family's first brain injury, so while I was thankful for the familiarity, I missed being able to talk to my mom.

This one evening, Mom sat in her chair in our front sitting room—the chair she had sat in every night for the past ten years at least. The news was on TV, also as usual. (Dad was a total news junkie.) I was at the kitchen sink with my back to the front room (where you can still find me most days, even now). Suddenly, Mom let out a sigh. Something about it sounded different, and I turned around to hear her say, "I want to go home."

"What did you say, Mom?" I needed to hear the words again because I thought I knew what she meant but just couldn't believe it.

"I want to go home."

It was striking how clear she was when she said it. There was no doubt. There was no fumbling for words. Home was no longer her house, her chair, her family. At that very moment, for her, home was the welcoming of death.

I wanted to scream, "No! Don't go! *This* is your home."

Instead I was, through the power of God, able to once again unclench my fists and receive this truth as a confirmation of her readiness, her willingness to hold even her life with open hands. It helped me encourage her as she grew much closer to death in those last days. To remind her that home was ready and waiting to welcome her. By accepting her fearlessness, I was able to encourage her later as I once again bore witness to death.

The women at the foot of the cross bore witness to the death of their Lord and friend, Jesus. They continued to follow his earthly journey beyond the cross, keeping careful watch over his body:

> The women who had come with him from Galilee followed along and observed the tomb and how his body was placed. (Luke 23:55)

> Mary Magdalene and Mary the mother of Joses saw where he was laid. (Mark 15:47)

As Joseph and Nicodemus placed Jesus's body in the tomb, they were not alone. The women stayed. Mary and Mary continued on, bearing witness to the burial of Jesus.

As a person who is admittedly familiar with death, I am also rather familiar with burials. The ceremonies and rhythms associated with wakes, funerals, and burials have also played a part of my bravely navigating the deaths around me. What I have learned through these ceremonies and rituals is that the rhythm of these traditions serves the living.

The procession goes from planning, to gathering, to remembering all milestones of a person's life, to a peace with death that those left behind can more easily grasp at the end of it all. After leaving my mom's funeral luncheon to bring home my newborn son, I knew that life continues on. Perhaps that's why I was willing to move mountains to get to my mother's funeral services. I knew that I needed the closure to peacefully forge ahead.

As I write this, we are just a few days away from gathering for my grandmother's services. She lived until she was 105 years old. This will be a celebration. We are eager to gather with family to remember and celebrate her life. Yet, admittedly, these days in between her death and our much-anticipated gathering feel a bit odd. We yearn for closure even with a death that has been joyfully welcomed.

The rituals of burial may honor the dead, but they serve the living.

The women, Mary and Mary, who bravely followed Jesus's body to the tomb, paved the way for the celebration of Jesus's resurrection. Because they fearlessly followed. Because they bore witness. Imagine how different it all would have been without them there?

Had the women not faithfully watched the burial, they would not have been witness to the resurrection. Mary Magdalene went to the tomb on Easter. She knew where to go because she was there when they buried him. Death pointed the way to life.

> Mary Magdalene and the other Mary were seated there, facing the tomb. (Matt. 27:61)

Good Friday ends with this one image: two women fearlessly facing death.

The death of Jesus leads to life for all. This is, of course, the ultimate lesson of Good Friday. May we fearlessly welcome death in our lives. Death to self, death to fear, death to all the things we are called to let go of so we may experience a life surrendered.

Via Dolorosa Way of Grief

As we follow Jesus from Gethsemane to Golgotha and then to the tomb, take a few moments to sit quietly with him. Similar to the Way of the Cross or Stations of the Cross, we will pause to reflect on the moments and meaning of Good Friday. There is grief in death. But there is also grief in our sin and in our misalignment with God. Before we continue on, we must pause and grieve.

REFLECT

- What do you see when you watch the women of Good Friday?

- How are they fearless?

- As you reflect, ask God to reveal his presence and will. What does he show you?

CONFESS

- Have you welcomed the death of control?
- Have you held on to fear?
- Where is there misalignment in your desires, actions, and thoughts?
- Where are you not valuing what Jesus valued?

RECONSIDER

- Letting go of our will and seeking God's will is the way to freedom, beauty, and life.
- The redemptive work begins with letting go of control.
- Take time to pray and affirm this.

POSTSCRIPT

BEAUTY IN DYING

Death of a Loved One

Good Friday is very much a story of losing a loved one—something I can very much relate to personally. When considering how we process the death of a loved one, we must wrestle with the reality that what we have (a loss) is not what we wanted. And with that, do we believe that God's goodness can be found in that loss? Jesus himself reminds us this is so.

After my dad passed, my children experienced their own period of mourning and grief, missing Osh, their grandpa. As a parent, I have been pressed to verbally assure my kids in new ways. They lost someone who they lived with every day of their lives. This was not like losing a distant grandparent. It was much, much more.

Their grief was deep and wide.

As my kids' grief settled in after six months or so, they started making connections between the grief they felt and the grief I must feel. Suddenly they realized I had lost all my parents. How could I be okay with this reality?

Lying in Max's bed one night, comforting him as he sobbed (not for himself but for me and my losses), I assured him I held peace about all of it. Such peace seemed unfathomable to him. It must have shocked him, because he pressed me to articulate how I was finally able to wrap words around the whole ordeal.

I had finally accepted that I just didn't know how things were going to go. I had believed God's best looked like my mom being present for my adulthood and my kids' childhood. I could imagine nothing better. So when that was not the story of my life, I experienced tremendous grief and loss. Now, twelve years later, I can say with assurance that I *am* living the life God designed for me, and that *is* best. I just didn't know what God's best would look like for me or for my family. I found peace once I surrendered to that truth. This is the ultimate surrender. We must get to the point where we want God's best for us even when it looks nothing like what we would call best. This is where abundant living is found.

In the hours prior to Good Friday, Jesus spoke to this. He told the disciples that he was going away, and that this was what was best *for them*. In John 16:7, Jesus said, "It is for your benefit that I am going away, because if I don't go away the Counselor will not come to you." Jesus is saying to them, "Something better is coming, better than you knew to hope for."

What if that is how we are meant to process loss? There is grief in the goodbye, but there can also be confidence in who God is and knowing that something better is coming. We may not know what it is or even to hope for it. But we can trust him with it.

As we become certain in our faith, bold in our proclamation, and fearless about death itself, we can see the beauty that comes from surrender.

When I share about what the last fifteen years of my life have entailed, it is overwhelming. There is loss after loss, trial after trial. I have shared some of it here, but there is still more that has happened than what is reflected in these pages. The road has not been easy.

Yet I know that each death, each trial has shaped me in profound ways—ways I am grateful for. My family and I have been forced, in the most kind and gracious way, to lean on God alone to get us through. Because of this, I know the beauty that comes from dying. I know the joy that comes from serving, the freedom found in not knowing the timeline. I know the abundance found in letting go of control.

In the final moments on the cross, Jesus shouted out, "My God, my God, why have you forsaken me?" (Matt. 27:46 NIV). These words can be easily misinterpreted. Where, at first glance, we may see Jesus despondent, the reality is he is quoting Scripture and confirming the glory to come. Psalm 22 begins with those same exact words: "My God, my God, why have you forsaken me?" (NIV). The psalm goes on in verse 22 to praise God, and then the last two verses offer a vision of what will happen after the resurrection:

> Their descendants will serve him;
> the next generation will be told about the Lord.
> They will come and declare his righteousness;
> to a people yet to be born
> they will declare what he has done. (vv. 30–31)

After quoting Psalm 22, the next words Jesus speaks, his last, are, "It is finished" (John 19:30).

Where the world may see despair, where we could easily feel despair, may we have the vision of the cross and remember that all is not as it seems. There is great provision found in loss.

Not everyone has the opportunity to be formed by Christ in such a way. Yet I think the path of following (and sometimes rolling with) God's will is, in some ways, far easier than trying to impose our own will to produce a desired outcome. In many cases, I felt like the extreme circumstances I faced had forced my hand. Things were fully out of my control, so releasing my white-knuckle grip was a non-issue. It was already done for me.

More than likely, this will not be your story. You will likely be faced with the decision to let go and trust God in small ways, every day. As our life has settled into a season of minimal "big" trials, it has been in the day-to-day decisions where I have had to surrender. Control creeps in quite easily here. I am continually humbled by what causes my fists to clench, what elements of control I continue to grasp for.

It is our joy and delight to serve the inner-city kids each Saturday alongside Mr. Tom. He is a particularly kind soul. He knows just how to connect with the most closed-off child in the group. I will often find him lying on the linoleum floor in the hallway of the basement we serve in, coaxing my own son out of his shell—drawing alongside him, asking questions, and simply, beautifully, being present. Mr. Tom is in no hurry. He arrives early; he stays late.

As we left one of the first Saturday afternoons and headed to our respective vehicles, I said, "See you at church tomorrow!" And Mr. Tom replied, in the most earnest way imaginable, "Lord willing!"

I thought about his response the entire car ride home. Well, of course we would see him the next day—we are both faithful attendees to the same church and neither of us had any other plans to prevent us from seeing each other at the 9:00 a.m. service the next morning. Why couldn't he just say, "Yes!" or "See you then"?

As I have gotten to know Mr. Tom over this year, I now know why. He holds tightly to Jesus and nothing else. He truly lives surrendered to whatever God has for him. So much so that in response to my question, his only possible response was "Lord willing," because Mr. Tom does not hold on to anything as a sure thing except that which is laid before him by the Lord. His posture toward what I perceived as a given challenges me in the best way.

I pray that we continue to welcome the deaths we are called to embrace—in both the big moments and the small moments. May we truly lay our lives in his hands and lay aside the need to control, to coerce, to command. May we surrender all in obedience to him.

This is the beauty found in death, in surrender.

His way is so much better.

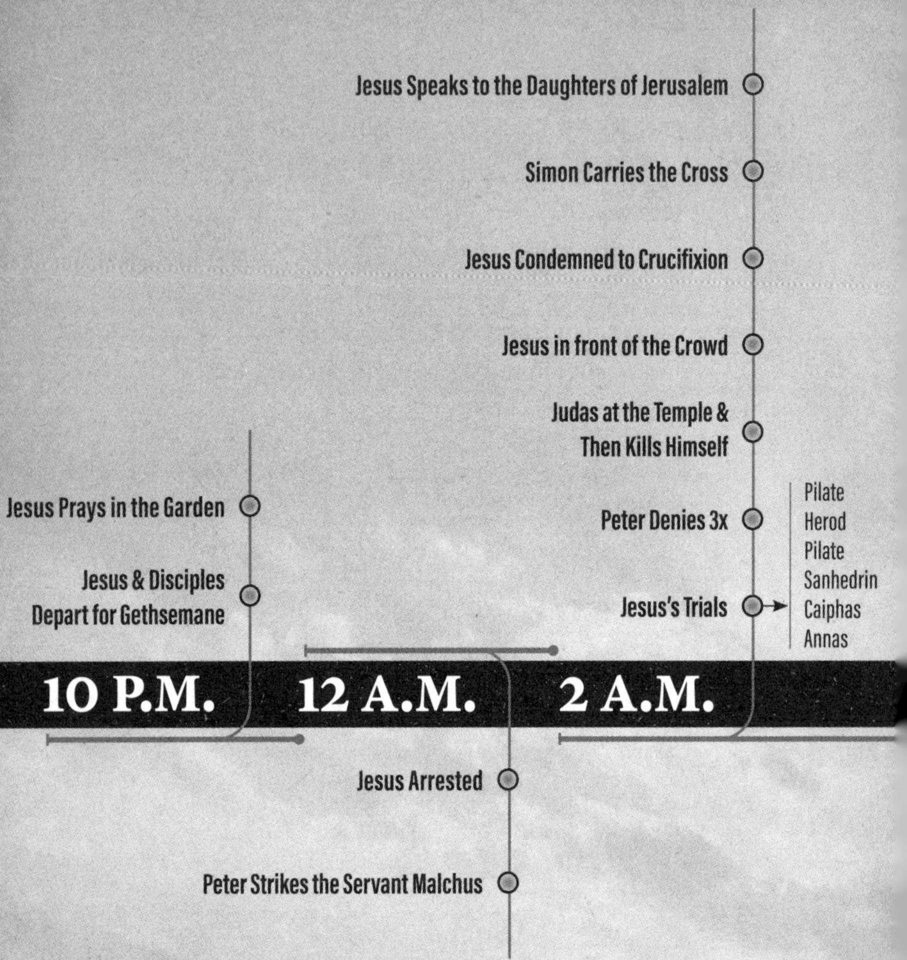

TIMELINE OF GOOD FRIDAY EVENTS

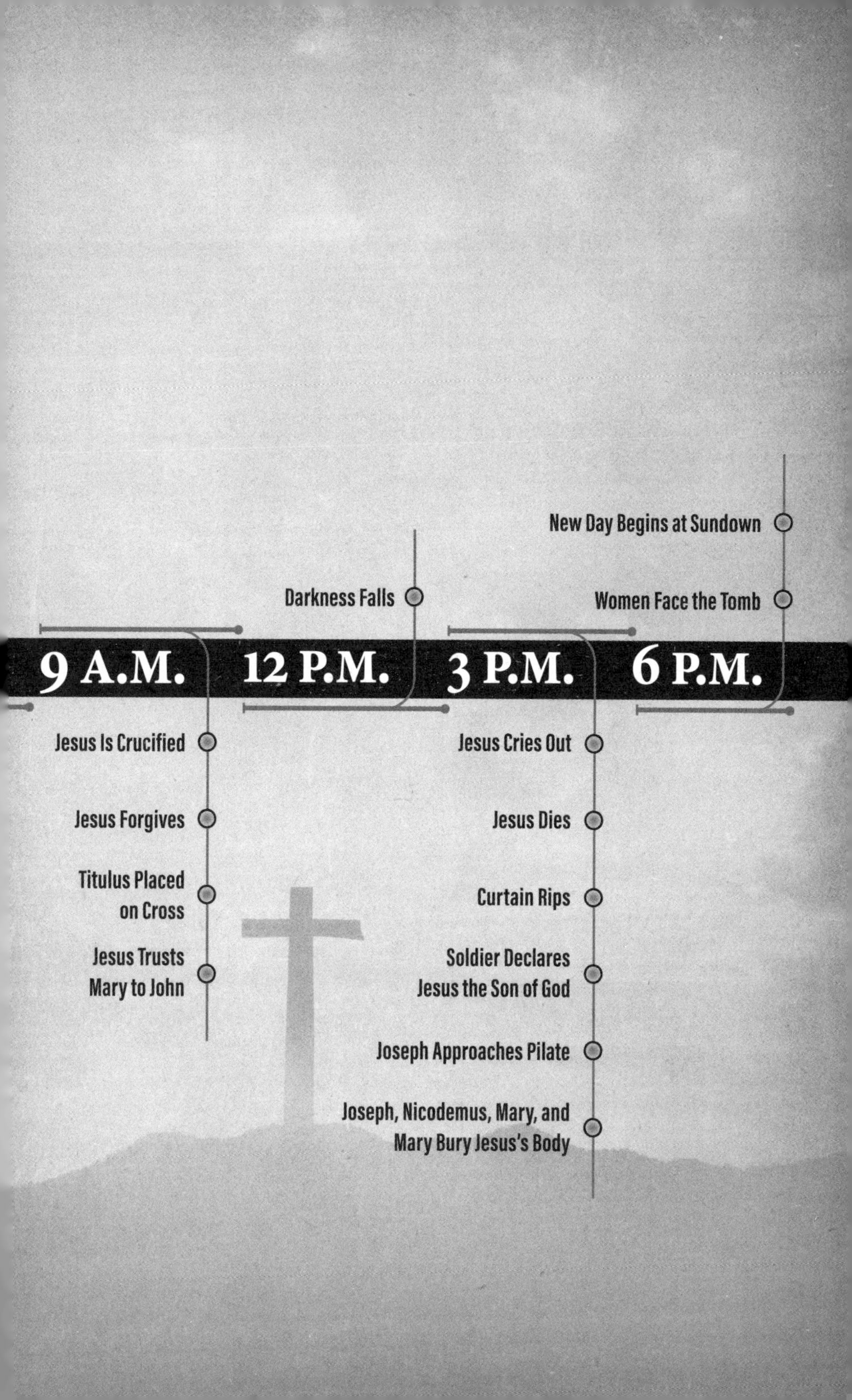
9 A.M.
Jesus Is Crucified
Jesus Forgives
Titulus Placed on Cross
Jesus Trusts Mary to John
12 P.M.
Darkness Falls
3 P.M.
Jesus Cries Out
Jesus Dies
Curtain Rips
Soldier Declares Jesus the Son of God
Joseph Approaches Pilate
Joseph, Nicodemus, Mary, and Mary Bury Jesus's Body
6 P.M.
Women Face the Tomb
New Day Begins at Sundown

WANT TO DIVE DEEPER?

Find a discussion guide, secret podcast, and detailed timeline of Good Friday on Jessica's website:

jessicaherberger.com/surrendered